TYPES OF PREACHERS
IN THE NEW TESTAMENT

D0062015

TYPES OF PREACHERS IN THE NEW TESTAMENT

BY

A. T. ROBERTSON, M.A., D.D., LL.D., LITT.D.

PROFESSOR OF NEW TESTAMENT INTERPRETATION,
SOUTHERN BAPTIST THEOLOGICAL SEMINARY,
LOUISVILLE, KENTUCKY

WAGGONER LIBRARY
DISCARD

BAKER BOOK HOUSE
Grand Rapids, Michigan

MACKEY LIBRARY
TREVECCA NAZARENE COLLEGE

Reprinted 1979 by
Baker Book House Company

ISBN: 0-8010-7607-2

PHOTOLITHOPRINTED BY CUSHING - MALLOY, INC.
ANN ARBOR, MICHIGAN, UNITED STATES OF AMERICA
1979

TO MY SISTER
JOSEPHINE ROBERTSON

PREFACE

These studies of some of the minor characters in the New Testament story illustrate the wealth of material in early Christianity. Human nature has infinite variety and perpetual interest. The author has already written books about the Baptist, Jesus, Paul, Luke, the Apostle John, Mark, and has one on the stocks about Simon Peter. So these are not included in this volume. The problem of the ministry is always a vital one and there are periods of pessimism about the ministerial supply. But God can use men of wide divergence in gifts and is not bound by any rules save those of life and love. The Word of God is not bound by any human shackles. The battle of the human spirit for fellowship with God in Christ goes on through the ages. A noble line of interpreters of Christ appear in every age.

A. T. ROBERTSON.

Louisville, Kentucky.

ACKNOWLEDGMENTS

Acknowledgments are made to the following journals for permission to reproduce chapters that had previously appeared in them: *The Biblical Review, The Expositor* (London), *The Methodist Review* (New York), *The Methodist Review* (Nashville), *The Christian Worker's Magazine, The Moody Monthly, The Expositor* (Cleveland), *The Record of Christian Work.*

CONTENTS

CONTENTS

TYPES OF PREACHERS
IN THE NEW TESTAMENT

CHAPTER I

APOLLOS THE MINISTER WITH INSUFFI-CIENT PREPARATION

The touch of genius does not belong to many. When a man of marked individuality confronts us, he at once attracts attention. We have various phrases that more or less conceal our ignorance of the subtle quality that charms us. We call it personal magnetism when we cannot otherwise distinguish the element of power. Apollos had the note of distinction. He was a marked man in any gathering and left his impress whenever he spoke. A man who could divide honours with Paul in Corinth is worthy of study. We are indebted to Luke (Acts 18:24-19:1) and to Paul (1 Cor. 1:12-4:21; 16:12; Tit. 3:13) for all that we really know about him. It is argued by some that he wrote the Wisdom of Solomon before becoming a Christian and the Epistle to the Hebrews after he learned to serve Jesus. But there is no real evidence for either theory. Paul calls him an apostle like himself, in 1 Corinthians 4:9, though it was true of him only in a general sense, since he had not seen the risen Christ and was not a personal follower while Jesus lived on earth.

A JEW WITH ALEXANDRIAN CULTURE

Luke speaks of him as "a certain Jew named Apollos, an Alexandrian by race." Schmiedel ("En-

cyclopædia Biblica") and McGiffert ("The Apostolic
Age," p. 291) seek to discredit the statements of Luke
in various particulars, but they admit this statement.
The Bezan text (D) gives the longer form of the
name, Apollonius. This is one of the few times that
Alexandria is mentioned in the New Testament,
though the influence of the Alexandrian teaching is
discernible in various passages, as in John 1:1-18;
Colossians 1:15-17; Hebrews 1:1-3. In Alexandria
the Septuagint translation of the Hebrew Bible was
made, and this Greek Old Testament exerted a tremendous influence on the Jews of the Dispersion and
upon early Christians. Alexandria had the greatest
library of antiquity and a great university. The Jews
were very numerous and were treated with much favour
there. Alexandria was thus a centre of Hellenism
and of Judaism. Plato and Moses met in Alexandria
in the Greek tongue. The Jews there read the Septuagint and spoke the vernacular *koine*. Thousands
of papyri fragments now reveal to us the Greek of
Egypt in the first century A.D.

One of the greatest Jews of all times lived in Alexandria in that century. Apollos could have studied,
or at least read, the philosophy of Philo, the chief
exponent of the Jewish-Alexandrian philosophy.
Grammar, rhetoric, philosophy, astronomy, mathe-
matics, medicine, geography, were all subjects of
lectures by learned professors in Alexandria. Apollos
lived in this atmosphere of culture and is thus like Paul,
who came from the environment of the University of
Tarsus. Christianity and culture have not always
understood one another. In some university circles to-

day Christ is taboo. The Renaissance led to the Reformation, but Erasmus and his Greek Testament did not hold all lovers of the new learning. Paganism still has its grip upon some modern scholarship. In Alexandria Philo sought to reconcile Plato and Moses. He did it by the allegorical method that won great favour in the later Christian school of theology in Alexandria under Origen and Clement of Alexandria. It was a favourite method of certain rabbis, and Paul is familiar with it. Apollos undoubtedly knew the new eclectic philosophy that combined Platonism, Aristotelianism, Stoicism, and Mosaism, and the new exegetical method. He was at home with the new rhetoric and knew how to express his opinions with force. Luke calls him "an eloquent man" ($\lambda\acute{o}\gamma\iota o\varsigma$), but the word means also "learned." In fact it includes both learning and eloquence (Knowling, Acts, *in loco*). The early Christians had none too many men of literary culture. Paul, Luke, and the author of the Hebrews are the outstanding ones. Apollos is a welcome addition to this small circle.

A MIGHTY INTERPRETER OF THE SCRIPTURES

Apollos was "able" ($\delta\upsilon\nu\alpha\tau\acute{o}\varsigma$) in the use of the Scriptures. A man may have a considerable knowledge of the Bible and yet not be able to use his knowledge effectively. But Apollos was no "Doctor Dry-as-dust." He did not have his learning laid away in an attic or in cold storage. He had learned much of the Old Testament by heart and knew how to find what he wanted. D. L. Moody was not as great a technical scholar as some men, but he knew how to use the sword of the Spirit with tremendous power; it was no Saul's armour to this David. Spurgeon was as remarkable for his knowledge of the Scriptures as for his skill as a preacher; his Treasury of David is a treasury indeed. Alexander Maclaren's "Expositions of Holy Scriptures" reveal the richness of Scripture knowledge possessed by this prince of preachers. John A. Broadus was another preacher of great pulpit power who gloried in the Scriptures. The last lecture that Broadus delivered to his New Testament class in the Southern Baptist Theological Seminary was on Apollos. He made a thrilling appeal to young ministers to be "mighty in the Scriptures."

It is not possible to be powerful in the use of the Scriptures without an adequate knowledge of the books of Scripture. One, if possible, should have technical acquaintance with the problems of scholarship, the language, the history, the religious ideas, the social conditions, the relations to other religions and peoples, the development in response to new ideas, the transforming power of Christ's life and teachings upon mankind. The word for "mighty" is used in Acts 7:22 of Moses, who was slow of speech: "And he was mighty in his words and works." He "was instructed in all the wisdom of the Egyptians." So was Apollos, only his Egyptian equipment included the addition of Hellenism and Judaism. Herodotus applies the word for "eloquent" ($\lambda\acute{o}\gamma\iota os$) to knowledge of history, and Plutarch uses it of eloquence (*Cf.* Knowling, Acts *in loco*). Ramsay ("St. Paul the Traveller," p. 267) calls Apollos "a good speaker, and well read in the Scripture." He is apparently the first

Christian preacher who expounds Christianity from the standpoint of the philosophy of Alexandria. Some Philonian speculations may well have been intermingled with his profound knowledge of the Scriptures. The allegorical method of exegesis would seem novel and wonderful, and the orator's touch gave a magic spell to his oratory. Such a man was bound to win a hearing and a following. As a loyal Jew he had devoted his learning and eloquence to the exposition of Scripture (Rackham, "Acts," p. 341).

A CHRISTIAN WITH ONLY THE KNOWLEDGE OF THE BAPTIST

Here we confront a difficult problem. Precisely how much did Apollos know of Jesus? The Bezan Text (D) says that "he had been instructed in the way of the Lord in his native land" (οὗτος ἦν κατηχημένος τὴν ὁδὸν τοῦ Κυρίου). This means that Apollos learned what he knew of Jesus in Alexandria. There is nothing impossible in that idea. The knowledge of Apollos may well represent the condition of Christianity in Alexandria when he left. Luke says that he knew "only the baptism of John" and yet he was "instructed in the way of the Lord" and "spake and taught accurately the things concerning Jesus." McGiffert ("The Apostolic Age," p. 291) says that this statement of Luke can hardly be accurate "because it seems contradictory." Schmiedel ("Encyclopædia Biblica") would make these verses later additions, and Wendt (Meyer, *Komm.* "Acts") would erase verse 25. Harnack ("Expansion of Christianity," i, 331n) says that "the whole narrative of Acts at this point is singularly coloured and obscure." There is obscurity, beyond a doubt, but it is not impossible to form an intelligent idea of what the theological standpoint of Apollos was when he came to Ephesus. It is not necessary to know whether he had learned what he knew of Jesus from a written document, one of the early attempts to set forth the work of Jesus (Luke 1:2). He may have had an early copy of Mark's Gospel if it ended at 16:8, as Blass suggests ("Philology of the Gospels," p. 31). Even if the word for "instructed" ($\kappa\alpha\tau\eta\chi\eta\mu\acute{\epsilon}\nu\sigma s$) implies oral instruction, as Wright argues (*The Expository Times,* Oct., 1897, p. 9f.), books were often read aloud. The point is not decisive. Catechists may have come to Alexandria, even though no Christian church may have existed there.

What we need to do is to approach Apollos from the standpoint of John the Baptist, not from that of Paul. John came "in the way of righteousness," Jesus said (Matt. 21:32). John was put to death before Calvary, before the Resurrection of Jesus, and before the great Pentecost. John went on with his work after Jesus began His ministry, but he clearly identified Jesus as "the Lamb of God, that taketh away the sin of the world" (John 1:29) and as "the Son of God" (John 1:34). He said that the Messiah would baptise with the Holy Spirit (Mark 1:8). He saw some of his disciples leave him to follow Jesus as the Messiah (John 1:37). John's work exerted a tremendous influence on Judaism, and it went on after his death. It is not strange that some of his disciples were caught in the transition stage and did not know all the rapid developments of Christianity. The

disciples of John who became Christians were not baptised again. John's baptism is all the baptism that
Jesus had, or His first six disciples. It was sufficient.
Baptism is probably used by Luke in Acts 18:25 for
the whole work of John as Jesus employed it in Matthew 21:25. Apollos, then, occupied the pre-Pente-
costal standpoint, though a sincere follower of Jesus
(Robertson, "John the Loyal," p. 293). He interpreted the things of Christ accurately as far as he
knew them. He had imperfect knowledge rather than
erroneous information. He was in no sense a heretic,
though he was sadly deficient in important points.

It is argued by some (Roberts, for instance, in
Hastings's "Dictionary of the Apostolic Church") that
Apollos not only "had an imperfect 'hearsay' acquaintance with the story of Jesus," but he really know no
more about Him than the twelve misguided disciples
of John whom Paul encounters in Ephesus after Apollos has gone (Acts 19:1-7). In fact these twelve
men are regarded by this theory as disciples of Apollos
and as an index of the knowledge possessed by him.
It is, I believe, wholly unlikely that these men were
disciples of Apollos, and, if so, they, as often happens,
failed to understand their teacher. Luke could not
have used the adverb "accurately" about the teaching
of Apollos if he knew no more than these twelve men.
They were ignorant of the Holy Spirit, of repentance,
and of Jesus. John the Baptist had taught all these
things, which, of course, Apollos knew. These men
were sadly misguided disciples of John whom Paul
instructs and baptises. There is no hint that Apollos
was baptised again. Luke contrasts their condition

with that of Apollos. These men were raw and un-
couth in their knowledge of the elements of Christianity. They represent the stage of some of the
disciples of John who hung on the very fringe of
Christianity. Apollos is much further along. He
lacked knowledge of the great events from the death
of Christ to Pentecost and the great missionary propaganda. It was a pity for so gifted a man to remain
with so limited a knowledge of Christianity. It is always a tragedy for a minister to be deficient in his
knowledge of the cross of Christ. Only the Spirit of
God can teach him fully.

A PASSIONATE ENTHUSIAST, QUICK TO LEARN

It is possible that Apollos first began to speak and
to teach privately, and then "he began to speak boldly
in the synagogue" (Acts 18:26) as Paul did afterwards for three months (19:8). Luke uses the same
word for this "bold" speaking by Apollos and Paul
($\pi\alpha\rho\rho\eta\sigma\iota\acute{\alpha}\zeta o\mu\alpha\iota$). It is employed in the New Testament only by Luke and Paul and always of the bold
declaration of the truths of the Gospel. Apollos did
not lack the courage of his convictions and was careful in his statements about Jesus to keep within the
bounds of his definite knowledge. This admirable
trait of minute accuracy is all the more noticeable since
Apollos was "fervent in spirit" ($\zeta\acute{e}\omega\nu\ \tau\tilde{\omega}\ \pi\nu\epsilon\acute{\upsilon}\mu\alpha\tau\iota$).
An enthusiastic temperament is sometimes exuberant
in expressions that are more florid and rhetorical than
accurate. Paul commends fervency (Rom. 12:11) as
one of the marks of sincerity. The word means literally boiling over (our "zeal").

It was in the synagogue that Apollos attracted the attention of Priscilla and Aquila, whom Paul had left in Ephesus when he went on to Cæsarea and Antioch (Acts 18:21f). The mention of Priscilla before Aquila here, though the Western and Syrian types of text have Aquila and Priscilla, may mean that Priscilla took the leading part in the further instruction of Apollos. They were evidently surprised and delighted with this remarkable preacher and saw at once the obvious defects in his knowledge of the Gospel. But they did not stop with this discovery, nor did they indulge in public criticism of the limitations of Apollos as an expounder of the faith. They could easily have closed the door of service for this brilliant man. But they apparently invited him home after worship, probably for dinner. "They took him unto them" (προσελάβοντο αὐτόν, indirect middle, took him to themselves).

Criticism is a delicate task, a sort of spiritual surgery, and, though greatly needed, is very difficult to perform without doing more harm than good. Preachers, like musicians, are highly sensitive, particularly about their sermons and their knowledge of the Gospel which is their specialty. Apollos had a great acquaintance with the Scriptures and philosophy and rhetoric. He was lacking in some important items about Jesus. It would have been easy to give him offence and to add to his eccentricity. But Priscilla was beyond a doubt a woman of tact. They "expounded unto him the way of God more accurately." This is simply superb. It was done thoroughly, neatly, and smoothly (ἀκριβέστερον αὐτῷ ἐξέθεντο). Fortunately they did not have to contravene any of his positions. He was correct as far as he went. Only he did not go far enough.

One can easily imagine how the heart of Apollos burned within him and how his eyes glistened as he learned of the Cross, the Resurrection, the Ascension, the Pentecostal Power of the Holy Spirit, the Gentile campaign for world conquest. He was an eager pupil and doubtless cheered the hearts of his hosts and teachers. Evidently Apollos exhibited profound gratitude for the new light that had been turned upon the great problems of Christianity. He readily saw the bearing of it all upon what he already knew so well. There is hope for the man who is ready to learn. One is never too old to learn. The minister who is always learning will always have a hearing. There is no dead line for him. That comes the minute one stops learning. Apollos is a rebuke to the preacher who is content to preach his old sermons through the years without reading the new books or mastering the old ones. Here is a profound student of the Scriptures, a master in Old Testament interpretation, who is glad to sit at the feet of Priscilla and Aquila and learn more of Jesus. That is the place for all of us, at the feet of anyone who can teach us more about Jesus. We cannot know too much about Him. We cannot be too accurate in our knowledge of Him. The passion of Paul in his later years was to know Jesus, for Christ always eludes us just a bit. There is always more to learn about the unsearchable riches of Christ.

A POWERFUL APOLOGIST FOR CHRISTIANITY

The Bezan text (D) has this: "And there were certain Corinthians sojourning in Ephesus, and when they heard him they besought him to cross over with them to their country. And when he had consented, the Ephesians wrote to the disciples in Corinth that they should receive the man." This is quite likely the real origin of the way that Apollos came to go to Corinth, though it is clearly not the original text of Acts. So Apollos "was minded to pass over into Achaia," and "the brethren encouraged him" ($\pi\rho\sigma\tau\rho\epsilon\psi$-$\acute{\alpha}\mu\epsilon\nu\sigma\iota$, putting him forward). He seemed to be just the type of man that would suit the situation in Corinth. Priscilla and Aquila knew Corinth well; and the Corinthian brethren in Ephesus no doubt felt that they had made a great "find" for their church in the metropolis, just like a modern pulpit committee. There was apparently no organised church as yet in Ephesus, though some Christians were there, besides Aquila and Priscilla. Apollos was fully equipped with a cordial letter of commendation. Paul will later comment on the fact that he himself needed no "epistles of commendation to you or from you" "as do some" (2 Cor. 3:1).

Apollos soon justified the wisdom of those who had brought him. "He helped them much that had believed through grace" (Acts 18:27). He seems to have addressed himself chiefly to those already Christians who had been converted under Paul's ministry. Evidently Apollos was less evangelistic than Paul. These hearers had already "believed through grace," and Apollos

"helped them much" ($\sigma\upsilon\nu\epsilon\beta\dot{a}\lambda\epsilon\tau o$ $\pi o\lambda\dot{\upsilon}$). He gave them
a constructive interpretation of Christianity with the
fresh glow of the new knowledge acquired in Ephesus
and, in particular, "he powerfully confuted the Jews,
and that publicly, showing by the scriptures that Jesus
was the Christ" (Acts 18:28). It will be recalled that
in Corinth the Jews had blasphemed Paul for preaching
this very doctrine (Acts 18:6) and had brought Paul
before Gallio, much to their sorrow (18:12-17). The
issue was still sharply drawn between Jews and Christians in Corinth. Apollos was doubly welcome because
of his great knowledge of and skill in the use of the
Scriptures. He "argued them down" ($\delta\iota a\kappa a\tau\eta\lambda\dot{\epsilon}\gamma\chi\epsilon\tau o$;
note imperfect tense and double compound). He did
not necessarily convince the Jews though he disputed
"vehemently" ($\epsilon\dot{\upsilon}\tau\dot{o}\nu\omega s$; *cf.* Luke 23:10).

But the powerful apologetic of Apollos made a profound impression upon the Christians in Corinth. He
was hailed, and rightly so, as a champion of the faith.
Apollos was a new type to them. The scholastic and
philosophical turn of his mind was pleasing in Corinth.
Paul did not have the excellency of speech from the
rhetorical standpoint or the persuasive words of wisdom (1 Cor. 2:1-4) that Apollos had and that many
of them liked. It is one of the blessings of life that
men have different gifts. God can use them all. It
would be a great misfortune if preachers were just
alike in intellectual equipment and in style of speech.

A SKILFUL BUILDER ON PAUL'S FOUNDATION

"I planted, Apollos watered; but God gave the in-
crease" (1 Cor. 3:6). Paul "as a wise master-builder"

(3:10; *cf.* Lock, "St. Paul the Masterbuilder") had
laid the foundation that should underlie every church,
Jesus Christ (3:11). "Another buildeth thereon," he
said, with probable reference to Apollos. Both Paul
and Apollos had been "God's fellow workers" (Θεοῦ
συνεργοί), while the Corinthian church was "God's
building" (Θεοῦ οἰκοδομή), "God's husbandry" (Θεοῦ
γεώργιον), to change the figure (3:9). Paul was the
architect (ἀρχιτέκτων), but he simply carried out God's
plan for the building. It required many men and
long years to build a cathedral which the German shells
demolished in an hour. But each man through the
years carried on the work according to the great plan
laid down. So Paul rejoiced in the work of Apollos
who succeeded him in Corinth, as Jesus rejoiced in
the work of John the Baptist who preceded Him (John
4:36f). The one who sows and the one who reaps
rejoice together. Each preacher enters into the labour
of others. There is no cause for jealousy, but only
ground for gratitude. It is part of the preacher's
business to learn how to fit his work into that of the
man who preceded him. He must be a constructive
builder, not a destructive critic. It is beautiful to see
how Paul rejoices in the work of his co-workers. He
had apparently not seen Apollos until he had finished
his work in Corinth and had returned to Ephesus
(1 Cor. 16:12).

We do not know why Apollos left Corinth. He may
have had premonitions of trouble. Divisions exist in
the church when Paul writes to them, that arose primarily out of partisan preferences for Apollos or Paul.
Weizsäcker ("The Apostolic Age in the Christian

Church," vol. i, p. 320) thinks that "an Apollos party was only formed some time after his departure. And this supposition is in turn confirmed by the fact that no shadow of blame fell on Apollos for the creation of the party." This judgment is in accord with the facts as we know them. We know nothing of the unfortunate schisms in Corinth, except what Paul tells us himself, save that the trouble was still there when Clement wrote his "Epistle to the Church." Paul recognises frankly the differences between his manner of preaching and that of Apollos. Men are not made after the same pattern. There are diversities of gifts from the same Spirit (1 Cor. 12:1-7). Apollos had rhetorical eloquence and used the language of the Alexandrian philosophy (wisdom), but Paul was not jealous of these gifts, since God had given him the demonstration and power of the Holy Spirit. Paul was their spiritual father, and Apollos could only be their pedagogue (1 Cor. 4:15). They had each his own place and work, and each would receive his own reward from God as steward of the mysteries of God (4:1-5).

It is evident that Paul regarded the work of Apollos as a continuation of his own, and he and Apollos were on excellent terms in Ephesus. The free way in which he uses his name shows this (1 Cor. 1:12; 3:4). Paul is not writing out of any jealousy of Apollos or of bitterness towards him. It is quite likely that Paul conferred with Apollos regarding the critical situation that had arisen in Corinth. They understood one another on this point (Kerr, "Int. Stand. Bibl. Encycl."). Apollos was no more responsible for the spirit of faction in Corinth than was Paul or Peter.

"Nor has he reproached Apollos with seeking to over-shadow him by his own mode and style" (Weizsäcker, *ibid.* p. 321). Paul tells us why he speaks so plainly about Apollos: "Now these things, brethren, I have in a figure transferred [μετεσχημάτισα] to myself and Apollos for your sakes; that in us ye might learn not to go beyond the things that are written; that no one of you be puffed up for the one against the other" (1 Cor. 4:6). This is the secret of the whole matter. "This sensitiveness on this point was directed not against Apollos but against the party" (Weizsäcker, *ibid.*). Paul speaks plainly that the schismatics may see the point. It was folly to split the church over three preachers (Paul, Apollos, Cephas) as they were doing (1 Cor. 1:12; 3:4), when these preachers were only co-workers and they could love them all (3:22f). Sometimes preachers are put in the light of opposition when they are wholly innocent.

A LEADER UNWILLING TO FOSTER A FACTION

Paul has some severe words about teachers who destroy the temple of God (1 Cor. 3:16-21). He undoubtedly has in mind the factional leaders in Corinth. It is bad enough when a man builds with wood, hay, stubble on the good foundation (3:12-15). Fire will test the quality of every preacher's and teacher's work. He may himself be saved, but all his preaching goes up in smoke, dry enough as some of it is. That is pathetic enough from the preacher's standpoint, but it is far worse for a preacher to be the cause of the ruin of a church. Some men are church-builders; others are church-destroyers and wreck church after church.

These men should be banished to a desert island. But
the best of men may be the occasion of strife in spite
of all that they can do.

After Apollos had left Corinth the members of the
church began to discuss the relative merits of Paul and
Apollos as preachers and teachers. The very eccen-
tricities of the two men were exaggerated and pitted
over against each other. Apollos' "brilliancy and
Alexandrian modes of thought and expression readily
lent themselves to any tendency to form a party, who
would exalt these gifts at the expense of Paul's studied
plainness" (Robertson and Plummer, "Int. Crit.
Comm.," p. 11). "The difference between Apollos and
St. Paul seems to be not so much a difference of views
as in the mode of stating those views; the eloquence
of St. Paul was rough and burning; that of Apollos
was more refined and polished" (F. W. Robertson).
But, after this issue was made partisans of each sprang
up and heat was engendered. It is possible that Peter
made a brief visit to Corinth, but at any rate the
Judaisers came and were only too glad to find opposition to Paul's leadership in Corinth. These men sought
to win the whole church away from Paul by playing
Peter against Paul and Apollos as the chief apostle
and the exponent of the real orthodoxy, free from the
Gentile laxness of Paul and the Alexandrian philosophy
of Apollos. This petty partisanship so disgusted some
that they actually made a partisan use of Christ's name
and started a Christ party (1 Cor. 1:12).

So the wheels went round, to the disgust of Paul
and of Apollos. The household of Chloe brought news
of the dreadful situation (1:11). Paul wrote in great

eagerness to quell the narrow spirit of selfishness before the church was ruined. He even begged Apollos
to go over and see what he could do (16:12), as some
of them may have requested: "But as touching Apollos the brother, I besought him much to come unto
you with the brethren; and it was not at all his will to
come now; but he will come when he shall have opportunity." Apollos was right to stay away, and not to
fan the flame by going back himself. He had not
caused the trouble; he would not add to it. Paul
himself is reluctant to go as yet (4:18f.). They both
set a good example for preachers when a church is
divided over the ministers. The world is wide and
Apollos went elsewhere. We last hear of him in Crete
as the bearer with Zenas the lawyer of Paul's Epistle
to Titus (Tit. 3:13). Some of the early writers say
that he went back to Corinth after some years; but it is
plain that Apollos and Paul continued to be friends.

A gifted man like Apollos is the very kind of man
to cause misunderstanding by his brilliant epigrams
and the charm of his style. One can only do the best
that he can and go on. But God has use for a brilliant scholar like Apollos, yes, and like Paul. Each
must do his work in his own way. If people praise
him, well and good. If not, "then shall each man
have his praise from God" (1 Cor. 4:5). "With me
it is a very small thing that I should be judged of you"
(4:3). Paul is not resentful or defiant in these words,
but he does hold himself above the petty scorn or praise
of the gossips in Corinth. The froth and the foam
pass away, but the name and the work of Apollos remain as part of the glory of Christianity.

CHAPTER II

BARNABAS THE YOUNG PREACHER'S FRIEND

One cannot resist the feeling that Barnabas is not properly rated by modern Christians. This defect is partly due to the fact that Luke does not trace his career after Chapter 15 of Acts. He drops from view under the shadow of the disagreement with Paul whose steps Luke traces all the way to Rome. And then we have no authentic writing of Barnabas. Tertullian and other writers in the West attribute to Barnabas the Epistle to the Hebrews, but the bare possibility of that theory is all that can be admitted. Clement of Alexandria quotes the so-called Epistle of Barnabas as the work of Paul's companion. Origen speaks of the Catholic Epistle of Barnabas and Eusebius mentions the Epistle of Barnabas. The Codex Sinaiticus gives it after the Apocalypse of John, showing that it was esteemed highly in Alexandria, and was read in some churches. But the writer is so hostile to the Mosaic law that it seems impossible to credit it to Joseph Barnabas. Some other Barnabas may have written it. McGiffert ("Apostolic Age," p. 598f.) pleads for the idea that Barnabas wrote 1 Peter, but not with convincing arguments.[1] We may pass by the

[1] Moffatt ("Introduction to Literature of the New Testament," pp. 343 n., 437) shows that Barnabas had no reason to conceal his authorship if he wrote the epistle.

Apocryphal Gospel and the Acts under the name of
Barnabas. The result is that we are left with no clearly
known writing of Barnabas by which we may measure
his life and teachings. We are wholly dependent upon
Acts and Paul's Epistles for our knowledge of this
great figure in early Christian history. There are
traditions that he was one of the seventy sent forth
by Jesus (Luke 10:1), that he preached the gospel in
Rome, that he was the founder of the Church in Milan,
that he worked in Cyprus till his death at Salamis in
A.D. 61. But Luke and Paul enable us to gain a clear
picture of Barnabas if we piece together all the inci-
dents wherein he figures. At the Conference in
Jerusalem (Acts 15:1-29; Gal. 2:1-10), assuming
the identity of the visits, the five foremost figures are
Paul and Barnabas on one side, Peter, James and John
on the other, in the private conference when the programme was drawn up and the concordat reached.
Lightfoot [1] hardly does Barnabas justice in his able
discussion of "St. Paul and the Three." Barnabas,
from this standpoint, is a mere figurehead. And yet
twice in Acts 15 the order is "Barnabas and Paul."
Barnabas spoke before Paul (15:12) as the better
known in Jerusalem and less offensive to the Church
there. In the Letter to the Antioch Church we read:
"our beloved Barnabas and Paul, men that have
hazarded their lives for the name of our Lord Jesus
Christ" (15:25f.). Elsewhere, save in Acts 14:14,
after Acts 13:43, Luke has it Paul and Barnabas.
Renan [2] pointedly says of Barnabas: "After St. Paul,

[1] "Commentary on Galatians," pp. 129-212.
[2] "The Apostles," tr., p. 124.

he was the most active missionary of the first century."
Renan [1] pleads that "Barnabas won at the hands of the
Christian world the highest degree of merit." Renan
would apparently rank Barnabas next to Paul. That
is too high a place for him when one considers John
and Peter. But he is entitled to stand with James, the
Lord's brother, in the group of foremost men of his
generation.

I.   A LIBERAL CONTRIBUTOR TO THE POOR SAINTS
IN JERUSALEM

It is in this capacity that we first hear of him (Acts
4, 36f.). His name is Joseph, but not the Joseph
Barsabbas Justus of Acts 1:23. His home was in the
island of Cyprus and, though a Levite, he owned property (probably there). Originally the Levites owned
no land (Num. 18:20), but the case of Jeremiah
(Jer. 33:7-15) shows that the rule was not always
strictly observed, for a Levite could buy or inherit a
piece of land. But in the new Christian community,
where most had little wealth, this Levitical irregularity
(Furneaux, "Acts," p. 68) may have stood in the way
of the influence of Barnabas. There was no compul-
sion, but the voluntary surrender of all for the good
of the whole at once gave Barnabas a place of prominence and power in the Jerusalem Church, to the envy
of Ananias and Sapphira.

Now Barnabas had shown himself the true Levite
with the Lord as his portion. He had spiritual wealth
(Rackham, "Acts," p. 63) that far outweighed the
value of his land. The use of the singular ($τὸ\ χρῆμα$)

[1] "The Apostles," p. 191.

implies that Barnabas gave the total value of the sale to the support of the poor saints, quite in contrast to the duplicity of Ananias and Sapphira. Our first picture of Barnabas is that of a man of generous sympathies with the common people in spite of his more aristocratic affiliations. He was a cousin of John Mark (Col. 4:10) whose mother, Mary, was likewise a woman of some wealth since her home in Jerusalem was the gathering place of the Jerusalem Christians (Acts 12:12).

It is probable that Joseph, the Cyprian Levite, identified himself thoroughly with the Jerusalem Church, and perhaps made his home with Mary. Luke mentions at this point the surname of Barnabas that was given him by the apostles, possibly at a later time, though his unselfish generosity already predisposed all to cherish the most kindly sentiments toward him.

Luke translates Barnabas by "son of exhortation" (υἱὸς παρακλήσεως), though the Greek covers also the ideas of consolation and of encouragement. There is no English word that can carry all these ideas, and we face the same difficulty with the term "Paraclete" for the Holy Spirit. Scholars are not agreed as to the etymology of the word Barnabas. The Aramaic *Bar* means son, and Nabas may be connected with the Hebrew *Nebi* (prophet), son of prophecy, or with the Aramaic *Nevahah,* refreshment. But Deissmann [1] argues that Barnabas is really Barnebous, Son of Nebo, a name found in a Syrian inscription. At any rate, there is no doubt that Joseph was worthy of the surname. He was a prophet and a teacher (Acts

[1] "Bible Studies," pp. 187f., 307-310.

13:1), and an apostle (Acts 14:14). He was worthy of all these titles, as we shall see. He was not one of the twelve, as Paul was not, but, like James the Lord's brother (Gal. 1:19), he was an apostle in the wider sense of the term. In the early years in Jerusalem Joseph Barnabas was a tower of strength for the young Church.

II. SPONSOR FOR SAUL WHEN UNDER SUSPICION

It may seem strange that the conversion of Saul was at most only a rumour in Jerusalem after the space of some three years. But Saul spent most of that time in Arabia, and his own conduct as the leader of the Pharisaic persecution in Jerusalem was enough to throw suspicion upon any reports of his change of heart and life in Damascus. Besides, the Sanhedrin may have spread sinister rumours about Saul's probable motives in his avowal of Christianity. His prolonged absence from Jerusalem was in itself peculiar, and he brought no letters of recommendation from the Christians in Damascus. It is not easy to live down one's past. The very completeness of Saul's work of destruction in Jerusalem made it all the more imperative that no mistake be made this time. The wolf might throw off the sheep's clothing and again ravin the fold. Saul had come "to visit Cephas" (ἰστορῆσαι Κηφᾶν, Gal. 1:18). He had not come to be inducted into his apostolic office. That authority he had received from the Lord Jesus, not from man (Gal. 1:1). But Saul wished to carry on his Gentile mission in harmony with the apostles, and there was much that he could learn about the earthly life of Jesus from Simon

Peter during these two weeks. It is probable that
Peter and Barnabas were both staying at the home of
Mary (Acts 12:12). No other apostles were present
in Jerusalem at the time save James the Lord's brother
(Gal. 1:19). Evidently Peter and James, as well as
the other disciples, were full of fear. "They were all
afraid of him" (πάντες ἐφοβοῦντο αὐτόν, Acts 9:26).
The imperfect tense pictures the shrinking away from
Saul as he presented himself. "He essayed to join himself to the disciples" (ἐπείραζεν κολλᾶσθαι τοῖς μαθηταῖς).
The imperfect tense. again shows that Saul did not
give up without a struggle. He was deeply mortified
beyond a doubt. "Saul's nature could ill brook mis-
trust; and there might have been unhappy consequences
but for the work of a mediator" (Rackham, "Acts,"
in loco). To put it bluntly, they did not believe that
Saul was a genuine disciple, not even his own repeated
statements to that effect. Saul stood discredited before
the very man whom he had come to visit as a brother
and co-worker. The memory of Saul's fierce hatred
of these men flared up like a flame. Criticism and fear
demanded that Saul furnish proof of his sincerity
before he be received as a brother in Christ. It was
a crucial moment for Saul and for Christianity. A
fatal misunderstanding at this moment might have
had the most disastrous consequences.

"But Barnabas took him (ἐπιλαβόμενος,, taking hold
of by the hand, literally) and brought him (ἤγαγεν,
perhaps with some reluctance now on Saul's part) to
the apostles (πρὸς τοὺς ἀποστόλους, face to face with
Peter and James)." Not simply did Barnabas do that,
but he "declared unto them how he had seen the Lord

in the way, and that he had spoken to him, and how
at Damascus he had preached boldly in the name of
Jesus" (Acts 9:27). Saul himself had told his story
to Barnabas, who now vouched for the correctness of
it and for the genuineness of his conversion. It was
a bold and a noble thing to do. It may well be that
Saul and Barnabas had been friends at the university
of Tarsus before they were Christians, the one a
Levite from Cyprus, the other the Pharisee from
Tarsus, both Hellenists and loyal young Jews. "It
was he who appreciated Paul; it was to him that the
Church owes the most extraordinary of her founders.
. . . Among the causes of the faith of the world we
must count the generous movement of Barnabas,
stretching out his hand to the suspected and forsaken
Paul; the profound intuition which led him to dis-
cover the soul of an apostle under that humiliated air;
the frankness with which he broke the ice and levelled
the obstacles raised.between the convert and his new
brethren by the unfortunate antecedents of the former,
and perhaps, also, by certain traits of his·character." [1]
This tribute to Barnabas is not overdone. The life of
Barnabas seems to be devoted to the ministry of those
in distress. It is a noble ministry for any life. Saul
and Peter and James could each tell how they had seen
the Risen Christ.[2] As a result of the friendship of
Barnabas Saul "was with them going in and going
out at Jerusalem" (Acts 9:28), received on terms of
perfect equality as the guest of Simon Peter. It is

[1] Renan, "The Apostles," p. 191.
[2] Swete, "The Appearances of Our Lord after the Resurrection," p. 88.

a high sort of courage to champion the cause of a discredited man. The Sanhedrin looked upon Saul as a
renegade Jew. The disciples feared him as a hypocrite.
Barnabas took him as a brother beloved and risked all
his own great reputation to save Saul to Christianity.
When the Hellenists in Jerusalem threatened to kill
Saul as he had led them to stone Stephen, "the brethren knew it," possibly Barnabas being the first to see
Saul's peril, and "they brought him down to Cæsarea,
and sent him forth to Tarsus" (Acts 9:30).

III. CHAMPION OF THE GREEK CHRISTIANS IN ANTIOCH

Events moved rapidly. The ministry of Philip in
Samaria led to the visit of Peter and John to investigate the work of grace among these half-Jews (Acts
8:14ff). The visit to Peter and the six brethren to
Cornelius (Acts 10), a God-fearing Roman and
proselyte of the gate in Cæsarea, made quite a stir
among the Pharisaic party in the Jerusalem Church
who called Peter to account for his mingling with the
Gentiles (Acts 11:1-18). But the word of God is not
bound, as Peter had found out though with difficulty.
Men of Cyprus and Cyrene went as far as Antioch
and "spake unto the Greeks also (correct text, in spite
of Aleph and B), preaching the Lord Jesus" (Acts
11:20). There was already a Samaritan Church from
Philip's work and a Roman Church in Cæsarea from
Peter's work. Now a Greek Church had sprung up in
Antioch, the third city of the Roman Empire. The
situation was a delicate one, and called for careful
handling. It is proof of the high position of Barnabas

in the Jerusalem Church that he was chosen (Acts 11 :
22) as a committee of one (cf. Acts 8:14) to investigate conditions in Antioch, for "a great number that
believed turned unto the Lord" (Acts 11:21). The
Pharisaic party in Jerusalem had acquiesced reluctantly
in what had happened in Cæsarea (Acts 11:18).
They were evidently alarmed at the sudden turn of
events in Antioch. Barnabas was himself from
Cyprus, and may have known some of the brethren
from the island. Besides, he was a Hellenist and so
better able to appreciate their feelings towards these
Greek Christians, perhaps proselytes of the gate like
Cornelius, while, as a Levite, he could be trusted to
understand Hebrew prejudices (Furneaux, "Acts,"
p. 173). All classes in the Jerusalem Church had confidence in Barnabas and in his ability to do justice to
the new movement and to decide whether it was of God.
Barnabas fully justified their choice of him as the
commissioner in this crisis. Luke pauses to bestow
a eulogy on Barnabas, quite out of his usual style.
It is possible that Barnabas was dead when Luke wrote,
"for he was a good man" (11:24), perhaps recently
deceased. At any rate Luke is fully aware of the significance of the occasion when Barnabas reaches
Antioch with the future of Greek Christians in his
hands. He knows what the Judaisers had tried to do
to Peter in Jerusalem. Barnabas exhibits consummate
wisdom at Antioch, and not the least element of his
wisdom is his staying there with the Greek Christians
and not returning to Jerusalem to make a report for
over a year. Barnabas at once saw that the work was
due to the grace of God, and he was glad (11:23).

"A smaller man would have raised difficulties" (Furneaux, "Acts," p. 173). But Barnabas was able to
rise above his Jewish prejudices and to recognise the
change wrought in the lives of these Greeks. He saw
that a new era had come and that God had broken down
the middle wall of partition and had saved these Greeks
without their becoming Jews. Barnabas was not the
man to lay the burden of Jewish ceremonialism on
these Christian freemen. So "he exhorted them all,
that with purpose of heart they would cleave unto the
Lord" (Acts 11:23). He kept on exhorting (παρεκάλει)
them, for reaction would come after the first enthusiasm of the new faith. Barnabas saw this peril, and
laid himself out to make the work of grace permanent
(προσμένειν).

He accepted the new order as a fact. He readjusted
his theology, if necessary, to suit the evident work of
God, as Peter had done at Cæsarea. But Barnabas required no vision on the housetop to see the new truth
that God is no respecter of persons (Acts 10:34). The
average Jew had the same pride of race that the Ger-
mans had before their defeat at the hands of the Allies.
Luke tells us how it came to pass that Barnabas was
able to see so clearly the hand of God in the spiritual
revolution going on in Antioch. "He was a good man"
(ἀγαθός, 11:24), a kindly and a generous man, who
was able to let the facts sweep away his prejudices.
He had convictions, but he was able to see facts that
contravened them and to accept them openly and
frankly. This is a severe test of character, and Barnabas stood it. He was "full of the Holy Spirit."
He was an inspired man in the true sense of that

phrase. He had the gift of *paraclesis* from the Para-clete. As a spirit-filled man, he was able to try the spirits and to discern the true work of grace when he saw it. He was a man "of faith," and so was able to trust God for the future of this work without undue restrictions on the liberty of the brethren. He accepted the Greek Christians as fully on a par with the Jewish Christians. The whole Church lived free from the Jewish ceremonial restrictions (Acts 15:1; Gal. 2:11-14). Barnabas was a son of exhortation, consolation, and encouragement to these Greek Christians.

IV.   FINDING A PLACE FOR SAUL IN ANTIOCH

The work grew mightily under the care of Barnabas. "And much people was added unto the Lord" (Acts 11:25). He saw that he needed help, and he knew where to go. He did not go to Jerusalem. He wished to bring no disturbing element into the life of the Greek Church in Antioch. Barnabas knew the man for this emergency. Tarsus was not very far from Antioch. Saul had not been idle during the years since he left Jerusalem in flight for his life. He had been preach-ing in Syria and Cilicia (Gal. 1:21). In his own way Saul had probably preached to the Gentiles in these regions and not without success, for we read of churches here at a later period (Acts 15:41). Bar-nabas believed in Saul in spite of his stormy career so far. He was sure that this man was a chosen vessel of God for this very work among the Gentiles. He determined to get Saul to Antioch so that the man and the hour could meet. I find it hard to believe that

the Church in Jerusalem had instructed Barnabas to
send for Saul if he needed his services.   It is rather
the insight into character that enabled Barnabas to see
that Saul was the master mind to meet this great crisis.
The door was open in Antioch for Saul, and Barnabas
"had none of the littleness which cannot bear the presence of a possible rival" (Furneaux, "Acts," p. 174).
The language of Luke implies that Barnabas was not
sure that he would find Saul in Tarsus, but he went
forth on this quest and found him and brought him
to Antioch (Acts 11:25f.).   The result justified the
wisdom of Barnabas.   He had blessed the church in
Antioch, and he had given Saul his great opportunity.
Renan overdoes the matter in saying that Saul "was
at Tarsus in a forced repose, which to an active man
like him was a perfect torture" ("The Apostles," p.
207), but Barnabas did forget himself and prepared
the field for the genius of Saul.   "All this is certainly
the very climax of virtue; and this is what Barnabas
did for Paul.   Most of the glory which is due to the
latter is really due to the modest man who led him
forward" (*ibid.*).   Barnabas and Saul had a happy
year in Antioch.   Here the disciples first won the name
of Christians, for they were not Jews and not heathen.
Finally Barnabas and Saul went to Jerusalem with a
generous gift from the Greek Church in Antioch to the
poor Jewish saints in Jerusalem (Acts 11:29f.) at the
time of the famine about A.D. 42-4.   The Judaisers
apparently made no protest, and the apostles were
seemingly absent when they arrived.   Barnabas had
saved the day for Greek Christians and had saved
Saul for his great work in the world.   "Thus twice

over did Barnabas save Saul for the work of Christianity" (Farrar).

V. ABLE TO TAKE SECOND PLACE FOR THE GOOD OF THE CAUSE

Barnabas maintained his position of leadership in Antioch on their return from Jerusalem (Acts 12: 25). In the great church at Antioch a democratic spirit prevailed. Five prophets and teachers are mentioned (Acts 13:1) apparently in two groups (τε—τε) of three prophets (Barnabas, Symeon called Niger, Lucius of Cyrene) and two teachers (Manaen, foster-brother of Herod the tetrarch, and Saul). The primacy of Barnabas is above dispute, and Saul comes last in the list as a newcomer, possibly the latest to join the band of leaders in Antioch. The other three may have been "the pioneers of Gentile evangelisation at Antioch" (Furneaux, "Acts," p. 191). They all three had Gentile affiliations. The five names represent five different countries, and too much difference between prophet and teacher is not to be insisted on here (1 Cor. 14:3). The same man could have both gifts. Luke is a true historian in preserving the proper perspective here. He does not allow Saul's future greatness to dim the glory of Barnabas, the real leader at this stage of the history of Christian missions. Dr. George Milligan (art. "Barnabas," Hastings's *D.B.*) illustrates how hard it is to preserve the historical perspective when he writes: "Barnabas accompanied Saul (or, as he was now to be known, Paul) on his first missionary journey." The Holy Spirit names the two men selected for the first great missionary campaign among the Gentiles with Barnabas as chief (Acts 13:2). This order is a matter of course with the Antioch Church, for no one at this date can challenge the positon of Barnabas in their esteem. They honour Saul and are glad to see him named as the lieutenant of Barnabas in the enterprise. The hearty prayers of the community of disciples go with the two great leaders as they are formally set apart to their special mission. We are not to think of this occasion as ordination to the ministry or to the apostolic office. Barnabas and Saul had long been fulfilling both functions. It is rather a prayerful dedication to the special task of the dangerous and unknown enterprise which they are undertaking like a farewell service to missionaries now. The Church at Antioch seemed to feel that it was a great step forward. There is no evidence that they undertook to finance the new departure, but they did agree for their two best leaders to go and their prayers went with them. There was no opposition and no saying that there were heathen enough in Antioch. It was a time of great spiritual enthusiasm when Barnabas and Saul, with John Mark as attendant, set forth upon their epoch-making journey. It is clearly Barnabas who took along his cousin John Mark. And yet before they leave Cyprus Saul (Paul) has leaped to the fore as the leader of the party. We shall never be able to explain precisely how it all happened. Beyond a doubt Paul was the abler man with more of the spark of genius. Barnabas was glad to have him use his great powers of speech in various emergencies. In a new environment Paul was no longer under the shadow of Barnabas's great reputa-

tion in Antioch. The case of Elymas was very pro-
voking as he tried to break the influence of Barnabas
and Saul over Sergius Paulus. Evidently Paul's
nature could stand it no longer. The explosive power
of Paul on this occasion (Acts 13:6-12) probably
amazed Barnabas and revealed the tremendous energy
of his fellow-labourer. There is no sign of resentment on the part of Barnabas as he sees his assistant
take the lead. After all Paul is the pride of Barnabas,
and he can rejoice that God has allowed him to bring
to the front this great exponent of the faith. Luke
quietly notes that "Paul and his company set sail from
Paphos, and came to Perga in Pamphylia" (Acts 13:
13). John Mark apparently disliked the new state of
affairs, and went back to Jerusalem, but Barnabas went
on with Paul. He was too great a man to break up the
partnership because Paul was manifestly the greater
and more useful preacher. "In nothing is the greatness of Barnabas more manifest than in his recognition
of the superiority of Paul and acceptance of a secondary place for himself" (Furneaux, "Acts," p. 203).
It was Paul who "stood up" in response to the invitation from the rulers of the synagogue to the "brethren" to speak in Antioch in Pisidia (Acts 13:15f.).
"Many of the Jews and of the devout proselytes followed Paul and Barnabas" (13:43) when the synagogue broke up. On the next Sabbath Paul was
again the speaker till the uproar came when "Paul and
Barnabas spake out boldly" (13:46). So they stirred
persecution against Paul and Barnabas (Acts 13:50).
At Lystra Paul was the speaker again (14:9), with
the result that the natives took Paul to be Mercury

and Barnabas Jupiter, a tribute to the finer personal appearance of Barnabas, as well as to Paul's eloquence as "the chief speaker." Here again Luke reflects the local atmosphere when he mentions "Barnabas and Paul" (14:14). But Barnabas apparently maintained his serenity, and the two apostles came back to Antioch with a glorious report of God's blessing. The door of faith had been opened to the Gentiles (14:27).

VI. EXPONENT OF GENTILE FREEDOM

It was a time of rejoicing in Antioch, and no doubt Paul's stature loomed larger in the minds of the Church there than before. When the Judaisers from Jerusalem appeared in Antioch with their abrupt demand that the Gentile Christians be circumcised after the custom of Moses (Acts 15:1) Paul and Barnabas took a firm stand against them. No doubt Paul revealed himself to the Church at Antioch as the real leader by his powerful exposition of liberty in Christ. This new appreciation of Paul appears in the appointment of "Paul and Barnabas" with certain others to go to Jerusalem for a conference on this grave problem (15:2). It is clear that the Greek Church at Antioch stood with Paul and Barnabas. In Jerusalem Barnabas nobly seconded the leadership of Paul with no sign of jealousy. It is here assumed that Acts 15 and Galatians 2:1-10 refer to the same event. The point is still in dispute, but the best reconciliation of minor discrepancies lies in the broad parallel of the two reports. Luke gives only the public aspects of the meeting, while Paul makes use of the private conference of the leaders to prove his equality with the

twelve. In Acts 11:30 "Barnabas and Saul" went to
Jerusalem. In Acts 15:2, "Paul and Barnabas"
attended the conference as in Galatians, and Paul is
evidently leader. In both reports (Acts 15 and Gal.
2) Peter and James co-operate with Paul and Barnabas. It shows Paul's wisdom that Barnabas spoke
before he did at the second public meeting (Acts 15:
12). In Jerusalem Barnabas had a great hold, and
he had here befriended Paul. This appreciation of
Barnabas is reflected in the decision of the conference,
probably written by James, which speaks of "our beloved Barnabas and Paul" (Acts 15:25), but Luke's
narrative in verse 22 has Paul and Barnabas. Paul
made no point of precedence. Barnabas stood by him
loyally in Jerusalem, and they won a common victory
over the Judaisers. But in his own account Paul said:
"to me and Barnabas" (Gal. 2:9).

But in Antioch on their return things did not go
entirely well. At first "Paul and Barnabas" taught
on as before (Acts 15:35) after the season of rejoicing over the Gentile victory. Paul and Barnabas had
been acknowledged by the Jerusalem leaders (Peter,
James and John) as in charge of the work among the
Gentiles, as they were at the head of the work among
the Jews (Gal. 2:7-10). Paul did not admit that
these "pillars" were above him and Barnabas. He
had made the issue acute in Jerusalem by the presence
of Titus, a Greek Christian, whose liberty was maintained against pressure for a compromise. Peter and
James spoke for Paul in Jerusalem. Later, so the
chronology seems to run, Peter came to Antioch and
followed the custom of Paul and Barnabas in his

social life with the Gentile Christians there (Gal. 2: 11-15). He ate with them. This was a long step forward for Peter, a Palestinian Jew, and the very issue on which he had been arraigned before in Jerusalem by the Judaisers (Acts 11:1-18). The reappearance of the Judaisers in Antioch with the threat to tell James about Peter and to have him up before the Church again quickly made a coward out of Peter. Social equality had not been passed upon by the Jerusalem conference. It was simply assumed here in Antioch. So Peter weakened and drew back. He was followed in this dissimulation (hypocrisy, Paul calls it) by "the rest of the Jews" till only Paul and Barnabas were left. And then one of the saddest things in Paul's life happened. "Even Barnabas was carried away by their dissimulation." There is a tribute to Barnabas in this way of speaking of his defection. Paul was now alone, *Paulus contra mundum.* But he did not waver. He spoke to Peter face to face, and seems to have won him back. Barnabas, of course, changed again to his old view. The breach was apparently quickly healed. But it is one of those things that can never be undone, once it has happened. Barnabas, like Peter, had flickered in this supreme crisis. The reins of leadership were, for the moment, left in Paul's hands alone. Paul could never quite forget that fact, nor could Barnabas nor could the church in Antioch. Paul was now undisputed leader of the Gentile Christians. But Barnabas had wrought nobly if he did falter for a moment when Paul and Peter called him to go different paths. Perhaps Barnabas "had never really thought out the principles involved, so as to be able to vindicate them when challenged" (Furneaux, "Acts," p. 248). It is possible also that John Mark, who was apparently now in Antioch (Acts 15:37), took the side of Peter against Paul with resentful memories of Perga (Acts 13:13), and so helped pull his cousin Barnabas away from Paul. It is plain that a sensitive situation exists in Antioch after Paul's triumph. There was plenty of explosive material at hand.

VII.   DEFENDER OF MARK'S RIGHT TO A SECOND CHANCE

Barnabas is true to his character as friend of the friendless to the end. Even in his inconsistent conduct at Antioch one may be able to trace the course of his conduct. He was a conciliating spirit always. He befriended the Gentile Christians, but he wished not to offend the Jewish brethren. So he faced a policy of vacillation. Perhaps in Antioch Barnabas was a bit restive under Paul's leadership after the recent honours shown him in Jerusalem. But Paul was all the more anxious to smooth things over and to get back to normal relations with Barnabas. The old missionary hunger burned in Paul again, and he proposed to Barnabas (Acts 15:36-41) that they go back again and visit their old haunts in Cyprus and Galatia. Barnabas readily agreed, even though he was to start out this time as Paul's assistant, not as chief. But he made one suggestion, that they take along with them ($\sigma\upsilon\nu\pi\alpha\rho\alpha\lambda\alpha\beta\epsilon\widetilde{\iota}\nu$, aorist infinitive) John Mark, who began the former tour with them. Instantly Paul took and held ($\check{\eta}\xi\iota o\nu$, imperfect) a position against that proposal. He could not bear the idea of having along (συνπαραλαμβάνειν, present infinitive, note) this man who had played the apostate (τὸν ἀποστάντα) at Perga. Mark did not stick to the work then (μὴ συνελθόντα αὐτοῖς εἰς τὸ ἔργον) and he might desert in a pinch again. Hippolytus calls Mark "the man with the finger wanting" (κολοβοδάκτυλος) because the Romans marked a deserter by cutting off the little finger. Paul's words stung Mark to the quick beyond a doubt, and all the more because of the truth in them. Probably Paul was indignant afresh at Mark for taking sides with Peter against him, and he disliked the suggestion of Barnabas all the more. The old sore has been rubbed again. There is more in the disagreement between Paul and Barnabas than can be put into words. The "sharp contention" (παροξυσμὸς, our "paroxysm") represented more than the conduct and character of John Mark. Barnabas now let loose the resentment at Paul's superseding him that he had smothered hitherto. Paul put into his resistance the passionate heat because of the dissimulation of Barnabas and of Mark. The "son of consolation" shows ordinary temper like other men. The apostle who later wrote the noblest hymn on love in existence (1 Cor. 13) is unable to control his own bitter thoughts. The dispute has come between these two men who owe so much to each other. The very debt of each to the other made the parting all the harder to bear. And yet each was right and each was wrong, as is usually the case in a quarrel. Barnabas had himself but recently made a false step in his relations with Paul and Peter. He was not the man to say that John Mark should be thrown to the scrap-heap for his slip at

Perga. A man is entitled to a chance to come back. No one of us is perfect, not even Paul. And yet Paul was unwilling to risk the work again with a man who had failed and had not yet made good. He demanded that he prove his mettle before he be trusted so much. There is no way to settle an issue like that. Paul no doubt had the best of the argument so far as logic goes, but Barnabas would not turn Mark down, not even for Paul. So they parted company, apparently abruptly. Barnabas took Mark with him and sailed away to Cyprus and drops out of Luke's narrative. It seems clear that the sympathy of the Church at Antioch is with Paul and Silas, who takes the place of Barnabas. Paul has completely ousted Barnabas in the affections of the Church at Antioch to which Barnabas had brought Paul. This is one of the tragedies of the ministry, that great men cannot always work together. But they can at least work separately. Often more work is thus accomplished. The world is wide and the work is pressing. Our hearts go with Barnabas in tender interest. One could wish that Luke had told us something of the closing years of Barnabas. Certainly he and Paul suffered because of the estrangement. There was no way to avoid that. But time heals many things. Neither of these great men was the man to cherish bitterness. We may be sure that Barnabas was not idle. He did a good turn by John Mark, as he had done by Paul. He helped to shape him for greater usefulness. When Mark appears later with Peter (1 Pet. 5:13) and Paul (Col. 4:10; 2 Tim. 4:11), he is useful for ministering to the aged Paul. This change in Mark is largely due to Barnabas, who befriended the young preacher in his hour of crisis. It is a great gift to be able to pick up and to patch up men. Barnabas knew how to do it. When men differed, he had to make his choice. But the great work that he did for Christianity in befriending Paul and Mark is a permanent contribution. That is his crown of glory, that and the Church at Antioch which was shaped by him and saved from the Judaisers for Paul's master hand. He began the missionary campaign that Paul carried to victory and that is still sweeping on over the earth. Paul clearly rejoiced in the later work of Barnabas, for he spoke kindly of him in 1 Corinthians 9:6. Luther and Calvin held that Paul refers to Barnabas in 2 Corinthians 8:18 f., "the brother whose praise in the gospel *is spread* through all the churches." This is pure conjecture, but it is plain that, like Paul, he supported himself while preaching, and had the same spirit of independent manhood. Christianity can never forget the work of Barnabas even though he does not reveal the genius of Paul and John. He was a man for a critical period of early Christianity and helped to tide over the transition from the Jewish to the Gentile phase of Christian activity.

CHAPTER III

AQUILA AND PRISCILLA PARTNERS IN SERVICE

"Loyalty" is a great word; according to Prof. Josiah Royce it is the greatest of all words. The World War made it shine with fresh splendour. Disloyalty is not only a vice, but a crime. Dr. John A. Hutton, of Glasgow, argues that "Loyalty" is "the approach to faith." It is the dominant trait in John the Baptist's relation to Jesus (see my "John the Loyal"). It is the outstanding characteristic of Aquila and Priscilla in their relation to Paul. We are not told much about them, but what is given by Luke (Acts 18:2, 18, 26) and Paul (1 Cor. 16:19; Rom. 16:3; 2 Tim. 4:19) sets this couple quite apart. "Aquila and Priscilla were, in St. Paul's eyes, people of importance in the early Church" (J. E. Roberts, in Hastings's "Dictionary of the Apostolic Church"). Paul speaks of them lovingly as "my coworkers" (τοὺς συνεργούς μου, Rom. 16:3) in language that "shows that Prisca and Aquila occupied a different position from that of Paul's other coworkers" Weizsäcker, "The Apostolic Age," vol. i., p. 394). He adds: "The Apostle distinctively set them side by side with himself. They had, indeed, from the beginning laboured along with him in a pre-eminent manner, and after they had already attested their worth independently." No group of Paul's friends would be complete that did not include those two interesting persons whose lives evidently played a prominent part in the history of early Christianity.

I. PRISCILLA'S PREËMINENCE

The manuscripts vary a good deal between the form Prisca and the diminutive Priscilla, both Latin. For the three passages in Acts the best manuscripts give Priscilla (the language of conversation), while the three in Paul's Epistle have Prisca, "the more courteous and correct form of her name" (Furneaux, "Acts," p. 293). Both Aquila and Prisca are Roman names, though Luke expressly says that Aquila is a Jew of Pontus (Acts 18:2). There is no reason to think that Luke is mistaken on this point, because the name Pontius Aquila occurs in connection with the Pontian family of Rome (*Cicero ad Fam.*, x. 33). There was a Jew of Pontus named Aquila in the second century A.D. who translated the Old Testament into Greek. It was common enough for Jews to have Roman names like Paul and Mark. Aquila could also have been a freedman, "as the greater part of the Jews in Rome were freedmen" (Knowling, "Acts," p. 383; cf. Schuerer, "History of the Jewish People," div. ii., vol. ii., p. 234). So Ramsay holds: "Aquila was probably a freedman. The name does indeed occur as *cognomen* in some Roman families; but it was also a slave name, for a freedman of Mæcenas was called (C. Cilnius) Āquila" ("St. Paul the Traveller," p. 269).

But it is not at all certain that Prisca (Priscilla) was

a Jewess. She may have been. Both of them could have been freedmen. One of the oldest catacombs of Rome is the *Cœmeterium Priscillæ* outside the *Porta Salaria*. De Rossi has shown that this cemetery "originates in the burying place of Acilius Glabrio and other members of the Acilian Jews" (Sanday and Headlam, "Romans," p. 419). "Priscilla" was a name that belonged to the Acilian Jews, as an inscription shows. So then both Aquila and Priscilla could have been freedmen of a member of the Acilian Jews. There is still another view. Plumptre ("Biblical Studies," p. 417) noticed that in four of the six places where their names appear the wife occurs first (Acts 18:18, 26; Rom. 16: 3; 2 Tim. 4:19). The usual theory is that this is due to the greater zeal, devotion, or ability of Priscilla. This may be true, probably was the case, but the New Testament says nothing about it. Hort ("Romans and Ephesians," pp. 12 f.) argues in favor of Plumptre's suggestion "that she was a Roman lady, of higher station than her husband, and that her position in Rome enabled her to render special services to the Church." Ramsay accepts this view also: "Probably Prisca was of higher rank than her husband, for her name is that of a good old Roman family" ("St. Paul the Traveller," p. 268). This view commends itself to me as the more probable in spite of the objections of Sanday and Headlam ("Romans," p. 420) that it is hardly likely that a noble Roman lady would travel around with a Jewish husband engaged in mercantile or artisan work. That all depends. If she had accepted Judaism, like many educated Roman women (*cf.* Josephus, "Antiquities,"

xviii. 3, 5), she would do so, especially when both had
become Christians. When in exile, besides, she would
be cut off from her income in Rome. If she was a
Roman patrician, she probably possessed considerable
means and was able to be of real service to Paul when
he was in Rome during his imprisonment, if she was
really there at that time. We know from the inscriptions that Christianity did penetrate into other leading
Roman families (Sanday and Headlam, "Romans,"
p. 420).

But even so it may still be true that "Priscilla was
a more active worker in the Christian Church than
her husband. In favour of this view is the statement
of Chrysostom (i. 306 D, 177 A, iii. 176, B, C) that
it was Priscilla's careful expositions of 'the way of
God' (Acts 18:26) that proved so helpful to
Apollos" (Tasker, in Hastings's "One-Volume Dictionary of the Bible"). So Harnack ("Expansion of
Christianity," vol. i, p. 79) speaks of "Prisca the
missionary, with her husband Aquila." At any rate
the unusual order of the wife before the husband must
be accepted as original, though in Acts 18:26 the
Western text has "Aquila and Priscilla." Harnack
has shown that the Western or B text of "Blass" is
"modified by an interpolator who objected to the too
great prominence given to a woman, and has made
the position of Priscilla less prominent" (Headlam, in
Hastings's "Dictionary of the Bible"). Ramsay
("Church in the Roman Empire," p. 101) notes that
the Western text likewise omits Damaris in Acts 17:
34. Ramsay thinks that this "order was, therefore, a
conversational custom, familiar in the company among

whom they moved; though it must have seemed odd
to strangers in later generations" ("St. Paul the Traveller," p. 268). But Priscilla had a worthy and noble
husband if she did excel him in some qualities. "They
are always mentioned together, both in the Acts and
in the Epistles, and they furnish the most beautiful
example known to us in the apostolic age of the power
for good that could be exerted by a husband and wife
working in unison for the advancement of the gospel" (McGiffert, "The Apostolic Age," p. 428). She
was the predominant personality, as is often the case,
and so is to be classed with Lydia and the other women
who laboured with Paul in the gospel. She shared
her husband's exile (Rackham, "Acts," p. 324) and
thereby won her greatest sphere of usefulness for
Christ.

Harnack ("Mission and Expansion of Christianity,"
i., page 79) has argued that Aquila and Priscilla wrote
the Epistle to the Hebrews, or, rather, that she wrote
it with the aid of her husband. There is a curious
interchange of "we" and "I" in the Epistle, but Paul
shows the same literary habit. Harnack thinks that
Priscilla's authorship explains the anonymity of the
Epistle, since in the second century there was strong
objection to the prominent position of women in the
apostolic age. Dr. J. Rendel Harris accepts it and
Marcus Dods says: "All that we know of Aquila seems
to fit the conditions as well as any" (Expositor's Greek
Testament, "Hebrews," p. 234). But, if Priscilla was
a Roman, it hardly seems likely that she could have
produced a book so Jewish and Alexandrian in style,
more after the order of Apollos. Besides, the mas-

culine singular participle ($διηγούμενον$) in Hebrews 11:
32 would not suit Priscilla. But she was gifted enough
for this or any other service.

II. BOTH VICTIMS OF ROMAN HATRED OF THE JEWS

Aquila is in Corinth, "lately come from Italy with
his wife Priscilla, because Claudius had commanded
all the Jews to depart from Rome" (Acts 18:2).
Suetonius ("Claudius," 25) expressly says that "the
Jews were expelled by Claudius for incessant riots
under a ringleader Chrestus (Christus)." The Romans could not distinguish between the pronunciation
of the *koine* Greek e and i. There is like confusion
in the manuscripts for "Christians" in Acts 11:26.
Christus may have been the name of a Jew in Rome
who caused the trouble, but it is likely that it is just
the Roman failure to preserve the real name Christ.
"Chrestus" in Greek is an adjective that means useful or worthy. If the reference in Suetonius is to
Christ, then Christianity enters into the disturbance in
some way. Perhaps the Jews and the few Christians
there, converts at the great Pentecost, had some disagreement and Claudius ordered them all off as Jewish
disturbers of the peace. The Jews had been brought
to Rome by Pompey in B.C. 61 and had been a constant cause of turbulence. Tiberius had actually sent
away four thousand Jews from Rome to Sardinia
with the hope that the malaria might kill them. However, Dio Cassius (lx. 6) explains that Claudius did
not actually drive the Jews out of Rome because they
were too many, over twenty thousand, but he "forbade them to hold the meetings enjoined by their

laws." Perhaps Claudius tried to execute his decree and did do so to some extent and for a short time. Some of the Jews did flee, Aquila and Priscilla among them, though the ban was later lifted so that they could return (*cf.* Acts 28:17). So Paul found Jews in Rome. The exact date of the decree of Claudius is not known. It is given all the way from A.D. 49 to 52. Ramsay holds that A.D. 50 is the correct date ("St. Paul the Traveller," p. 254). On this showing this interesting couple did not arrive in Corinth more than six months before Paul came from Athens. It is curious how bitter race prejudice was between Jew and Gentile. In A.D. 41 a man named Heraclides was in many difficulties. Serapion writes to him: "Beware of the Jews" (καὶ | σὺ Βλέπε σατὸν ἀπὸ τῶν 'Ιουδαίων, B. G. H. 1079, l. 24). This scrap of papyrus throws light on the decree of Claudius just a few years later. Alas, hatred of the Jews has not yet disappeared from the earth.

III. EARLY MEMBERS OF THE CHURCH IN ROME

On this point one cannot be dogmatic, but it is difficult to keep from having an opinion, though the material is not sufficient for positive knowledge. What is clear is that Aquila and Priscilla could tell Paul "of the events that had occurred in Rome at the action of Chrestus" (Ramsay, "St. Paul the Traveller," p. 255). We know that Paul later (Acts 19: 2) announced a purpose to see Rome, and this plan may be due to Aquila and Priscilla. The silence of Luke in Acts 18, is argued both ways. It is strange, Knowling holds, that no mention is made of the con-

version of Aquila and Priscilla if they were Christians
when Paul met them. On the other hand, Rackham
thinks that the ready inference is to be drawn that
they were already Christians, since otherwise Luke
would have mentioned their conversion and baptism
as in the case of Lydia. The truth is that we do not
know. Milligan (Hastings's "Dictionary of the
Bible," "Aquila") comes near the probable truth when
he says: "The ready welcome which Aquila accorded
to one whom the bulk of his fellow-countrymen viewed
with such disfavour as Paul, inclines us to the belief
that when he came to Corinth he had at least accepted
the first principles of Christian faith, though his progress and growth in it he doubtless owed to the apostle.
If so, he and his wife may be ranked amongst the
earliest members of the Christian Church at Rome;
and it would be from them that Paul would learn those
particulars regarding the state of that Church to which
he afterwards refers in his Epistle (see Rom. 1:8, 16:
17-19)." Knowling admits the possibility that Jews
from Rome were at the great Pentecost who could
have carried the knowledge of Christ to the Eternal
City, and that but for some leanings to the new faith
Aquila and Priscilla would hardly have admitted Paul
to their lodgings. Claudius thus played a great part
in the life of Aquila and Priscilla in driving them to
Corinth into the fellowship of Paul, who became the
great friend of their whole lives.

IV. COMRADESHIP WITH PAUL IN CORINTH

Luke says of Paul that he came to Aquila and Priscilla and that, "because he was of the same trade with

them, he abode with them, and they wrought; for by their trade they were tentmakers" (Acts 18:3). The word employed here by Luke for "of the same trade" (ὁμότεχνον) is a classical word, though not in the Septuagint. Hobart ("Medical Language of St. Luke," p. 239) argues that this is a technical word for fellow physicians (so used by Dioscorides). At any rate there were trade guilds in plenty during the first century A.D. Edersheim says: "In Alexandria the different trades sat in the synagogue arranged into guilds; and St. Paul could have no difficulty in meeting in the bazaar of his trade with the like-minded Aquila and Priscilla (Acts 18:2, 3), with whom to find a lodging" ("Sketches of Jewish Social Life," p. 89). It was the Jewish custom to teach all boys a manual trade, one that the great war has shown to be exceedingly wise for both boys and girls. Jesus was by trade a carpenter and Paul a tentmaker. Tent-making was a flourishing local industry in Tarsus. The rough goats' hair, called cilicium from Cilicia, was employed in making tents for which there was a great demand all over the East, as is still the case. This boy learned to make tents, to study philosophy at the University of Tarsus, and theology at the feet of Gamaliel in Jerusalem. Pontus, like Cilicia, was "a district with abundant pasturage for goats and numbered tent-making amongst its industries" (Furneaux, "Acts," p. 292). So these two Jewish Christians were both tentmakers (σκηνοποιοί). It was hard to cut the rough cloth straight, but Paul learned it as he did the straight interpretation of God's Word (2 Tim. 2: 15). Aquila and Priscilla were now working at this trade because they had been driven out of Rome and were now away from their income. Paul had already worked at his trade to support himself at Thessalonica (1 Thess. 2:9; 2 Thess. 3:8). Probably Aquila and Priscilla had opened a shop and they took Paul in as a partner in the business. At any rate Paul lived in their house (ἔμεινεν παρ' αὐτοῖς) and they worked steadily at their business (ἠργάζοντο, imperfect tense). Dr. Samuel Cox has a chapter on "St. Paul a Workingman and in Want" in his "Expositor's Note-Book," pp. 419-438. But there was more than comradeship in trade between these choice spirits. He found also a Christian home which refreshed his soul after the cold indifference of Athens, and he "established a link with the Church in Rome" (Rackham, p. 329). Paul worked for his living with his own hands and preached as occasion came in the synagogue on the Sabbath and "tried to persuade (ἔπειθεν) both Jews and Greeks" (Acts. 18:4). This was his habit of independence (1 Cor. 9:12, 15; 2 Cor. 13:13). "No man should be able to say that he cared more for the fleece than for the flock" (Furneaux, p. 295). It was a blessed copartnership, and Aquila and Priscilla learned from Paul the art of winning souls to Christ and of training them for his service. They were already expert tentmakers. They now became expert evangelists. Aquila and Priscilla step into the background when Timothy and Silas come from Thessalonica to Corinth (Acts 18:5). They brought so much help that Paul was able to preach more and make fewer tents συνείχετο τῷ λόγῳ), with the result that the Jews were soon aroused to anger by Paul's tremendous success. After some two years in Corinth, Aquila and Priscilla accompany Paul to Ephesus (Acts 18:21). Either Paul or Aquila had a vow which was absolved at Cenchreæ and they went on. In the light of Acts 18:19 it seems as if Aquila and Priscilla sought to establish themselves in business in Ephesus and wished Paul to go in with them as in Corinth: "And he left them there; but he himself entered into the synagogue and reasoned with the Jews." The point is not clear, but Paul meant to go on to Cæsarea and to Jerusalem (apparently) and then to Antioch (18:22). He planned, however, to come back to Ephesus and rejoin Aquila and Priscilla if it was God's will (18:21). So Aquila and Priscilla were left by Paul in a city with few, if any, Christians besides themselves. Thus they began in Corinth also. They would make tents as at Corinth and as Paul later did on his return to Ephesus: "Ye yourselves know that these hands ministered unto my necessities, and to them that were with me" (Acts 20:34). So Paul spoke to the elders from Ephesus at Miletus of his work in Ephesus with Aquila and Priscilla. But we may be sure that Aquila and Priscilla would be on the lookout for every opportunity to serve the cause of Christ.

V. SKILL IN TRAINING A YOUNG PREACHER

We do not know how long Paul was absent from Ephesus. Luke says that he spent "some time" in Antioch (Acts 18:23) before he started on the third missionary journey. Paul was certainly away some months, since he also "went through the region of Galatia and Phrygia, stablishing all the disciples"

(18:23).   He probably arrived at Antioch in the
spring and at Ephesus in the autumn of A.D. 53 or
54. Ramsay ("St. Paul the Traveller," p. 266) thinks
October the probable month.   It is clear that during
Paul's absence Aquila and Priscilla would carry on
their trade and do what they could to win converts to
Christ.   There was pretty clearly no church as yet
in Ephesus.   After Paul came back he preached for
three months in the synagogue (Acts 19:8f.) till
compelled to leave for the school of Tyrannus.   Luke
gives us only one item in the experience of Aquila and
Priscilla as they did pioneer work during Paul's absence.   It is the visit of Apollos to Ephesus and how
Aquila and Priscilla took him in hand.   Ramsay thinks
that Luke records this incident "not so much for its
own intrinsic importance as for the sake of rendering
Paul's first letter to the Corinthians clear and intelli-
gible.   A contrast is drawn there between the more
elaborate and eloquent style of Apollos and the simple
gospel of Paul; and it is implied that some of the Corinthian brethren preferred the style and gospel of
Apollos.   The particulars stated here about Apollos
have clearly been selected to throw light on the circumstances alluded to, but not explained in the letter
("St. Paul the Traveller," p. 267).   Perhaps so.   At
any rate the passage serves that purpose for us whether
or no it was the specific design of Luke.   I think that
the incident has great value and interest in itself both
in the career of a man of unusual gifts like Apollos
and in the attitude of Aquila and Priscilla toward this
remarkable young minister who has suddenly come
across their path.   Ephesus was one of the great cities

of the world and men came thither from everywhere with all sorts of beliefs (Oriental cults, Hellenism, Judaism). The great Temple of Diana was the pride and glory of Ephesus. Aquila and Priscilla laid the foundations for Christianity in Ephesus. They were naturally concerned about everything that affected the cause. They still worshipped in the synagogue with the Jews and doubtless spoke to the Jews and to the "God-fearers" among the Gentiles who came. Apollos of Alexandria also spoke in the synagogue (Acts 18: 26). He did it with such boldness, novelty, and power that a real sensation was made. He preached Jesus, and yet not precisely as Aquila and Priscilla had learned him from Paul. They saw at once that such a man would do great good or great harm. He could not be ignored. He must be an ally or an opponent. It is a great gift to be able to judge men. It was clear that Apollos with all his Alexandrian philosophy and eloquence was right on the main things in Christianity as far as he went. He still tarried at the place held by John the Baptist. He needed instruction rather than denunciation. Christian leaders have not always known how to treat a new voice that begins to interpret Christ in a new day. Some go wild over the novelty of manner or the very defects of the man and exaggerate these into error or eddies of truth. Others fiercely rail at the newcomer for his theological shortcomings and vagaries and try to drive the strange voice away. Nowhere is more wisdom required than in the training of preachers both young and old. Aquila and Priscilla saved Apollos for the cause of Christ by wisely leading him into fuller knowledge of Christ. It

is not always easy to teach a gifted man and to correct
a sensitive man's defects. Priscilla and Aquila did it
privately and Priscilla probably did the most of it
with a woman's deftness and adroitness. It was a
noble service to render and points the way for us all
to-day when scholarship and Christianity are not always harmonious. There is a middle ground between
heresy and obscurantism. The cure for error is more
truth. Apollos erred by defect, but he was eager to
know more. Roberts (Hastings's "Dictionary of the
Apostolic Church") raises the question whether the
elementary and chaotic state of things in Ephesus at
this stage did not make Aquila and Priscilla more than
willing to urge Apollos to pass on to Corinth, where
his philosophical turn would have a riper audience.
Something is to be said for this view, though one
doubts if they were uneasy that the eloquent Alexandrian might overshadow them in Ephesus. Ramsay
is puzzled as to how the twelve mistaken disciples of
the Baptist had escaped the knowledge of Apollos and
Aquila and Priscilla before Paul came ("St. Paul the
Traveller," p. 270). But Ephesus was a large city
and had many elements in its population.

VI. MAKING THEIR HOME A CENTRE OF CHURCH LIFE

When Paul writes to Corinth he says: "Aquila and
Priscilla salute you much in the Lord, with the church
that is in their house" (1 Cor. 16:19). Thus we
know that a church was established in Ephesus before
Paul writes this letter and that one of the meeting
places was the home of Aquila and Priscilla. It was
the habit of this noble couple. They gathered Chris-

tians to their home. When Paul writes to Rome he sends salutations to the church in the home of Aquila and Priscilla (16:5). The disciples had to worship where they could, in synagogue, school, home. This couple used their means to make a home for the followers of Christ. It was a primitive arrangement, but it had some advantages. It carried worship into the home, and that is a great blessing. Family worship is now a rare spectacle. What would Christianity have done in the first century but for access to homes like those of Mary in Jerusalem, Cornelius in Cæsarea, Lydia in Philippi, Justus in Corinth, Aquila and Priscilla in Ephesus and Rome? There were probably other such meeting places for the Christians in Ephesus and Rome (*cf.* Rom. 16:14f.). But this item shows that they did their work in Ephesus well. It requires more courage to bring Christ into the home than to attend church. The presence of Christ in the home comes closer to our bosoms and touches our business life. If our homes were centres of active Christian influence, a revolution would come in the world.

VII. RISKING THEIR LIVES FOR PAUL

In Romans 16:4 Paul speaks of Priscilla and Aquila "who for my life laid down their necks." The language is bold and picturesque. Literally it means that they laid back their necks (τὸν ἑαυτῶν τράχηλον ὑπέθηκαν) for the ax of the executioner. It is probably not to be taken literally any more than Paul's language about fighting with wild beasts at Ephesus (1 Cor. 15:32). These wild beasts were men like the mob that gathered in the amphitheatre at Ephesus and

clamoured for Paul's blood. They were like the beasts
in the gladiatorial arena. Paul was not allowed by
his friends to go to this gathering of the mob, but it
is quite possible that Aquila and Priscilla were caught
in the maelstrom of their rage when they seized Gaius
and Aristarchus, "Paul's companions in travel" (Acts
19:29). Paul was so indignant at this wanton act
that he wanted to go and face the mob. It took the
disciples and the Asiarchs to hold him back (19:
30f.). It is possible that at this juncture, as Paul was
living with Aquila and Priscilla, they volunteered to
go and face these wild beasts and try to dissuade them
from their murderous intents toward Paul, just as
courageous spirits have stood before a mob engaged
in the crime of lynching and endeavoured to restore
them to reason. At any rate Aquila and Priscilla took
their lives in their hands and risked all "for my life"
(ὑπὲρ τῆς ψυχῆς μου). They were ready to die to save
Paul's life. This great sacrificial act Paul could never
forget. It set Aquila and Priscilla apart among Paul's
friends. They were henceforth knit together by this
blood bond. The fact that they escaped with their
lives in no wise decreased Paul's sense of obligation to
them for their heroic deed. It was loyalty to the limit
and Paul cherished the memory of their courage.

VIII.   GOOD TRAVELLING CHRISTIANS

The last mention of Prisca and Aquila by Paul is in
2 Timothy 4:9. Timothy is in Ephesus and is requested by Paul to salute this devoted couple. It has
been objected that for this and other reasons Romans
16 does not belong to that Epistle, but should be

added to the Epistle to the Ephesians or to a lost
Epistle. It is said that the life of Aquila and Priscilla
is pictured as too nomadic—now in Rome, now in
Corinth, now in Ephesus, now in Rome, now in
Ephesus. But Lightfoot ("Biblical Essays," p. 299)
replies that a nomadic life was precisely the characteristic of the Jews of that day. Paul's own life is a
case in point. We know why Aquila and Priscilla left
Rome for Corinth and Corinth for Ephesus. It is not
hard to see why they would be glad to go back to Rome
when the way was clear. They may have returned to
Ephesus on a mission for Paul. Their migratory
habits furnish presumptive evidence for the integrity
of Romans (Tasker, Hastings's "One-Volume Dictionary of the Bible"). That Paul had so many acquaintances and friends in Rome before he went there
himself is not strange. Everybody went to Rome
sometime or other who could manage it. The travelling habits of Jews and others explains the rest. Paul
had met these people here and there. They are now
in Rome. As to Ephesians we know that it is a circu-
lar letter to several churches in Asia and not designed
for Ephesus alone. Priscilla and Aquila were Paul's
"fellow workers in Christ Jesus" whether in Corinth,
Ephesus, or Rome. Paul is grateful to them, but many
others also feel the same way, "all the churches of the
Gentiles" in fact (Rom. 16:4). Here we catch a
glimpse of the missionary zeal of this couple. They
were known and loved, Paul says, through Gentile
Christendom. They were great travellers, but they
took Christ with them wherever they went. Like
Abraham of old, they set up an altar to the Lord in

every city. It is a discredit to many that they are not
good travelling Christians. Our modern globe-trotters
care much more for sight-seeing than for hunting up
disciples of Jesus in out-of-the-way places. In every
city in America there are thousands of people who
were active Church members in the country or town
before they moved to the big city. Now they wander
from church to church or drop out entirely. They
do not carry with them the same activity for Christ
that they displayed at home. Place it to the credit of
Aquila and Priscilla that they made a business of their
religion. It was not an appendage to be left off in
travelling. There took Christ with them all the time.
Harnack thinks that this was chiefly due to Priscilla,
whom he considers a sort of female apostle in her
zeal. "Plainly the woman was the leading figure of
the two, so far as regards Christian activity at least.
She was a fellow labourer of St. Paul—*i. e.,* a missionary—and she could not take part in missionary work
or in teaching, unless she had been inspired and set
apart by the Spirit. Otherwise, St. Paul would not
have recognised her. She may be claimed as ἡ
ἀπόστολος, although St. Paul has not given her this
title ("The Mission and Expansion of Christianity,"
ii., p. 66). At any rate, it is easy to see how useful
to Paul and to the cause of Christ Priscilla and Aquila
became. They were welcome visitors anywhere in the
world where Jesus was loved. They could ply their
trade and push on the kingdom of Christ, fine speci-
mens of lay preachers, business people who were thoroughly independent as to their own support and yet
who made their lives count tremendously for the work

of Christ. They were self-supporting missionaries who rejoiced in the privilege of giving all to Christ. They were rich in their friendships and in their service. They enriched the lives of thousands and endeared themselves to Paul, who lived with them two years in Corinth and three years in Ephesus and who had tested their love for Christ to the core. They carried their business sense and social prestige into the service of Christ and employed both as weapons in the warfare which they waged for righteousness.

CHAPTER IV

JAMES THE MAN OF POISE

I. JAMES THE BROTHER OF JESUS

Paul refers to "James the Lord's brother" (Gal.
1:19). Peter sent a message "to James and to the
brethren" (Acts 12:17). Jude describes himself as
the "brother of James" (Jude 1). The author of the
Epistle of James terms himself "James, a servant of
God and of the Lord Jesus Christ" (James 1:1).

It is evident that we have here one and the same
man and that he is not James, the son of Zebedee and
the brother of John, slain by Herod Agrippa I (Acts
12:1, 2), and not one of the twelve apostles. There
is no reasonable doubt, therefore, that in Acts 12, 15,
21 we are dealing with the author of the Epistle, the
brother of Jesus.

Scholars disagree as to what is meant by the term
"brother." The natural meaning is that he is the
son of Joseph and Mary, the eldest of the younger
brothers and sisters of Jesus mentioned in the Gospels
(Mark 6:3; Matt. 13:56). The names of the four
brothers are given (James, Joses, Judas, Simon).
Since Jesus was not the actual son of Joseph, James
was the half brother of Jesus.

Some hold that these brothers and sisters of Jesus
were step-brothers and sisters, children of Joseph by
a former marriage. Others contend that brother and

sister really here only means "cousin." There is a full discussion of the whole matter in Mayor's "Commentary on James" and a brief one in my "Practical and Social Aspects of Christianity." I hold that James was the son of Joseph and Mary.

II. BLINDED BY THE LIGHT

It seems that at first James and the other brothers of Jesus were proud of his work at Cana for they were in frank fellowship for a while in Capernaum (John 2:12). There was apparently no estrangement at this time (Patrick, "James the Lord's Brother," page 46).

We are not able to trace the origin of the suspicion and distrust that finally arose in the Nazareth home. Mary understood the destiny of Jesus, but the brothers and sisters probably reflected the popular resentment in Nazareth on the occasion of his visit there (Luke 4:16-31). At any rate they appear by and by to think that Jesus is "beside himself" (Matt. 12:46f.; Luke 8:19f.) and wish to take him home.

The Pharisees had openly charged that Jesus was in league with the devil and even Mary for the moment feared that the excitement had unbalanced him. Later the brothers of Jesus offered cynical advice to Jesus about his Messianic work (John 7:5-10), advice that he took pains to disregard.

It is plain, therefore, that Jesus was misunderstood in the home circle at Nazareth, though his mother was loyal to the core and to the end.

It is not unusual for those who live at the foot of a mountain to take little interest in the glory and grandeur of the peak. Contemporaries of the great are

proverbially unable to gauge rightly the standing of
the men or their age. We see but one section of the
facts and are too close to the mountain to see its true
perspective. The flies at night beat their lives out
against the electric light, blinded by the light. The
Light of the world shaded his light in the home circle
beyond a doubt.

There was no posing and no professionalism, but
James knew Jesus as his elder brother, the carpenter,
and probably was unable to see what it was that suddenly lifted him to the place of a rabbi, and a prophet,
and miracle worker and finally of the long-expected
Messiah. One need not be unduly severe upon James
to see how the problem puzzled him.

III. WON TO THE LIGHT

Evidently James was drawn to Jerusalem by the
events of the Passion Week. Luke calmly notes that
the brothers of Jesus with their mother form part of
the goodly company that meet in the upper room and
wait for the promise of the Father (Acts 1:14).

Evidently a complete change has come over the attitude of James. Paul explains how it came to pass by
the appearance of the risen Christ to James (1 Cor.
15:7). We have no details of that meeting, probably
in the city somewhere, though it may have been in
Nazareth.

But James was not a man to hold out against the
facts. Undoubtedly he preferred to believe in his
brother as the Messiah and Lord if the facts justified
him in doing so. He probably felt keenly the shame of
the Cross, for Jesus had died as a condemned criminal.

It required a piercing ray of light to drive away the fog of doubt and distress from the mind of James. We may be sure that Jesus dealt tenderly with James as he did with Thomas. The position of James was difficult. Like Nicodemus at first he could not comprehend the new ideas of the Kingdom. Now after the death of Jesus it all seemed like a wild dream that was over.

Perhaps James grieved most because of the anguish and disappointment of his mother. But Jesus knows how to touch the mainspring of each heart whether it be Nathanael, Thomas, James, or Saul. Dale, indeed, thinks that James was converted before Jesus manifested himself to him ("Epistle of James," page 5). Mayor ("Commentary," page xxxvii) is disposed to believe part of the legend of Jerome about James being at the last Passover meal. We do not need to fill out the story. James saw Jesus. Henceforth he called himself a "slave of the Lord Jesus Christ." He was in the upper room with the hundred and twenty and was at home with the disciples.

IV. THE LEADERSHIP OF CHARACTER

One may wonder why James was not chosen to succeed Judas instead of Matthias. His kinship to Jesus would naturally give him prominence, but James had not companied with the disciples from the first (Acts 1:22).

And yet we soon see James in the lead in the Jerusalem church. Paul singles him out as one that he saw on his visit to Peter (Gal. 1:18, 19). Even Peter on his release from prison sends a message to "James and the brethren" (Acts 12:17).

At the Jerusalem conference (Acts 15:1-35) James presides, makes the closing address, and writes the decree of freedom for the Gentiles. Paul in Galatians 2:9 recognizes James as one of the pillars of the church in Jerusalem on a par with Peter and John. On the occasion of Paul's last visit to Jerusalem James is still the leader of the church there (Acts 21:17-26).

There is no doubt about the fact of the leadership of James. He came to hold the chief position in the Jerusalem church whether a chief elder, or pastor, or apostle.

It is not clear what title he had. At first he probably won his way by force of character. He was a man of mark as the brother of Jesus, but so were the other brothers of Jesus now in the church. James forged ahead by sterling qualities that fitted him for the part in Jerusalem.

After the death of Stephen and the conversion of Saul, the twelve apostles were increasingly absent from Jerusalem in their work of evangelisation. James was regarded as a thorough Jew and leaned to the Palestinian outlook rather than to that of the Hellenistic Jews like Stephen and Barnabas. His conservatism won their confidence when the peril of Gentile Christianity first appeared. The party of the circumcision looked to James to put a stop to what Peter had done up at Cæsarea (Acts 11:1-18).

V. A MAN OF PRACTICAL WISDOM

He came to be called James the Just, but his Epistle reveals him as James the Wise. The date of the Epistle is in dispute. In general, one may say that it was written before the Judaising controversy arose (before 50 A. D.) or after it died down in the second century (M. Jones, "The New Testament in the Twentieth Century," page 321).

Ropes ("International Critical Commentary," page 51) thinks that the writer's smooth Greek style makes it unlikely that it was written by James the Lord's brother, though it probably belongs to the period 60 to 70 A. D. But the vernacular κοινή was a flexible tool and responded to the personal equation.

There is no allusion to the points at issue between Paul and the Judaisers. This is all the more striking since James employs some of the very words in debate between them (faith, works, justification). But he fails to touch what Paul has in mind. "Paul is looking at the root; James is looking at the fruit. Paul is talking about the beginning of the Christian life; James is talking about the continuance and consummation. With Paul, the works he renounces precede faith and are dead works. With James, the faith he denounces is apart from works and is a dead faith" (Hayes, "International Standard Bible Encyclopædia").

James writes in the atmosphere of the Sermon on the Mount and is not thinking of the developed theology of Paul that was sharpened by the Judaising controversy. Both believe in faith as the way of salvation, both believe in works as proof of faith.

James in his Epistle perceives echoes of the teaching of Jesus. He has many figures of speech like those of Jesus. He was in very truth much like Jesus. It is not improper to say that both had a common inheri-

tance from Mary their mother. Hayes notes also that
James was called a just man as was Joseph his father
(Matt. 1:19). They breathed the same home atmos-
phere.

It is possible that some of the aphorisms of James
come from Mary. At any rate his Epistle is the chief
wisdom book of the New Testament. It is not ab-
stract philosophy, but practical wisdom applied to
actual conditions in private and social life. The
Epistle is modern in its treatment of cleanness of personal living and justice between employer and em-
ployé. Sociological problems are boldly faced and
are solved in the spirit of Christ and of human brotherhood. One can find in the parables and sayings of
Jesus the same courageous fairness that James dis-
plays. Pungent paradox and crisp epigram occur in
the teachings of Jesus and of James.

It has often been noted that the speech of James
and letter to Antioch in Acts 15 closely resemble in
style the Epistle of James. He was clearly a man of
ability, of poise, of spiritual reality, of energy, of leadership. He knew how to meet actual conditions and
to apply the gospel to the life of his time. It was a
great thing for the church in Jerusalem to have as pastor such a man. No one was so well qualified as he
to write a message to Jewish Christians at large concerning the evils that threatened their Christian life.
No man's words would carry more weight in the dec-
ade between 40 and 50 A. D. when he probably wrote
his book of wisdom.

VI.   JEW, BUT NOT JUDAISER

It is probable that the reactionary party in the Jerusalem church claimed James as one of them.   We
know what they did when they appeared in Antioch
after the Jerusalem conference and attacked Peter for
his social commingling with the Greek Christians there
(Gal. 2:11-14).

It is possible, of course, that James may have dis-
approved of this social freedom on the part of Jewish
Christians, though he was opposed to the Judaisers in
their controversy with Paul.   But the fact that James
expressly disclaims (Acts 15:24) responsibility for or
connection with the attack of the Judaisers on Paul
and Barnabas at Antioch makes even that unlikely.
Probably James had kept quiet at the time when Peter
was arraigned by the party of the circumcision (Acts
1:1-18) and when the controversy first arose at Antioch.   He was not a man to take a position rashly.

But, if the Judaisers had counted on James, they
were sadly disappointed.   Paul tells us how he made
certain that James and Peter and John were not led
astray by the Judaisers (Gal. 2:1-10).   There is a
certain amount of heat in Paul's vigorous narrative
which is written to prove his equality with and independence of the twelve apostles.   The vehemence is
partly due, at any rate, to the conduct of the Judaisers
in Galatia.   And yet in the private conference that
Paul had with the leaders in Jerusalem there was demand on the part of some of the timid brethren that
Paul yield in the case of Titus, the Greek brother,
whom he had brought with him.   If so, they would

agree for Paul to have freedom for the other Gentile
Christians. It is not said by Paul that James, or Peter
or John, took that view and wished Titus to be circumcised. But compromise was suggested by some.
In the end Peter, James, and John shook hands with
Paul and Barnabas as their equals in authority and
agreed to full Gentile liberty.

There is a trace of irritation in Paul's tone of reference to these "pillars." It is possible that they held
back from openly taking Paul's side till they had
heard the whole story. Paul makes it clear that he
does not consider that their agreement with him made
his cause one whit more right than it was before.
Still, he was glad to have the open support of the
Jerusalem leaders.

In the open conference after this private discussion
the schedule went through all right. Peter championed the cause of Paul and Barnabas. James spoke
last and with convincing force showed by the Scriptures how the Gentiles were included in the plan of
God. He suggested that the Gentile Christians take
pains to avoid idolatry, impurity, and murder or blood
(according to the Bezan text). But he was wholly
opposed to placing the yoke of Jewish ceremonialism
upon the necks of the Gentile Christians. It is small
wonder that the Jerusalem church voted unanimously
with Paul and Barnabas after such a deliverance from
James, the president of the conference.

James appears in the finest light on this occasion
and rendered a great service to the cause of spiritual
freedom for all time. He was cautious and prudent,
but reliable in a pinch. He had the courage to stand

up boldly for the evangelical faith in the teeth of the Judaisers who had counted upon him to lead their forces against Paul. If he had done so, Christianity would at once have divided into Jewish and Gentile factions. The crisis was averted by the fact that James stood with Paul.

VII. HIS FATEFUL ADVICE TO PAUL

Montgomery (Hastings's "Dictionary of the Apostolic Church") thinks that James merely approved the action with which Paul was greeted on his last visit to Jerusalem (Acts 21:17-26). Who the spokesman was is not clear, though James himself (Rackham) would be the natural man. The elders had met at the house of James (πρὸς Ἰάκωβον 21:18) to pay their respects to Paul. Probably the apostles were all absent from Jerusalem.

It is not necessary to regard the advice given Paul as a rebuke to Paul. The implication is plain that James and the elders did not believe the accusation of the Judaisers circulated so diligently and persistently (dinned into people's ears, κατηχήθησαν 21:21) that Paul taught Jewish Christians not to observe the customs of the fathers and taught apostasy from Moses by the Jews. Furneaux thinks that "the whole tone of the narrative implies that Paul was coldly received." I do not see it that way, for Luke expressly says that "the brethren received us gladly" (21:17).

The company that thus greeted Paul so heartily was probably small in comparison with the body of the church, but "St. Paul found himself a brother amongst brethren" (Knowling, "Commentary" in loco). The spirit of the formal meeting of the elders on the next day was cordial and friendly.

We must bear in mind that Paul had come to Jerusalem this time with a heavy heart and against the advice of many friends. He probably observed due caution on his arrival (Hort, "Judaistic Christianity," page 106). (Acts 21:4, 11-14). Paul went from a strong sense of duty (20:22-24). He must finish his course and face the issue in Jerusalem even if it meant his death (21:13).

He had long seen the gathering cloud in Jerusalem. The Judaisers had not lived up to the agreement of the Jerusalem conference. They had dogged Paul's steps and injured his work in Galatia, Achaia, Macedonia, Asia. They had persistently misrepresented Paul's attitude. He had fought for and had won liberty for Gentile Christians from the burden of Jewish ceremonialism. He had held to the moral observances of the moral law as a proof of conversion, but had refused to impose Moses on the Gentiles as a means of salvation. He had not waged war on the Jewish Christians. He was one himself and felt at perfect liberty to observe the Mosaic rites.

In fact, Paul had celebrated the Passover at Philippi (Acts 20:6) and had made a point to get to Jerusalem in time for Pentecost (20:16). He had come to bring alms to the Jewish Christians from the Gentile Christians of Achaia, Asia, Macedonia, Galatia to show their love and to cement the bonds between Jewish and Gentile Christians so as to avoid a schism (Rom. 15:22-33).

It was proposed that Paul be seen in the temple

offering sacrifices and paying for them. Actions speak louder than words. If the Jerusalem disciples see Paul in the Temple offering sacrifices and paying the charges of the four brethren who are discharging a vow, that will be the end of all controversy on the point of Paul's real teaching.

Was the advice of James wise or unwise? The way to answer that question is to keep clear in one's mind the purpose of the proposal. The object of the advice was to prove to the rank and file of the Jerusalem church that the Judaisers had misrepresented Paul's attitude toward Jewish Christians.

Did the plan accomplish its purpose? There is no evidence that it did not. To be sure, trouble grew out of the execution of the plan, but not from the Judaisers and not from the Jerusalem Christians.

Paul delivered the alms that he had brought to the church and spent a whole week in the fulfilment of the sacrificial offerings (Acts 21:27). It would seem that the full purpose of the proposal was attained. In all the entanglements that follow no trouble comes from the Jerusalem church or from the Judaisers. It would seem, therefore, that the advice was sound and wise. The peril of schism was averted. The reinstatement of Paul in the confidence of the Jerusalem church was apparently complete. The attack that was made on Paul while engaged in worship in the Temple (Acts 21:13-22) came from Jews of Ephesus (Asia) who had hated Paul there and who were angered by seeing him in Jerusalem (not the Temple) in company with Trophimus, a Greek Christian of Ephesus.

It was Jewish hate that exploded against Paul in

the Temple, an echo of the riot in Ephesus. This attempt to lynch Paul by the Jews was made while Paul was finishing the proposal of James, but it might have come anyhow on some other occasion. It had no necessary connection with what Paul was doing. In fact, he was in the very act of honouring the Temple when these Asian Jews accused him of dishonoring it. We may well decide, therefore, that James did not lose his reputation for wisdom and for sincere friendship towards Paul by the outcome of his advice.

VIII. THE VICTIM OF JEWISH HATE

And James himself, like Paul, was to fall a victim of the very Jews whom he so sincerely loved and tried to help. We may pass by the highly coloured story of Hegesippus, in Eusebius, that James was hurled from the pinnacle of the Temple to his death because he refused to renounce and denounce Jesus at the demand of the scribes and Pharisees. But Josephus ("Antiquities," XX; IX:1) has a sober narrative of the death of James.

The testimony of Josephus is no longer pushed lightly aside. Festus was dead and Albinus had not yet arrived. So Ananias (son of the Annas of the Gospels) assembled the Sanhedrin "and he brought before it the brother of Jesus who is called Christ (his name was James) and some others, and delivered them to be stoned, on a charge of being transgressors of the law."

And this was the treatment accorded the Jewish Christian who was so strict a Jew that the Judaisers had claimed him as belonging to them. Hegesippus says of his pious exercises: "His knees became hard like a camel's because he was always kneeling in the Temple, asking forgiveness for the people."

The Jews, the rich Jews (Pharisees and Sadducees), had killed the righteous one (James 5:6), the brother and Lord of James. They likewise killed James the Just (Righteous) in a fit of passion because of his love for and loyalty to Jesus.

Stephen was the first martyr who followed in the steps of Jesus. Many quickly followed in his train. James, the son of Zebedee, soon drank his cup of death (Acts 12-1, 2). In due time James, the brother of Jesus, took his place among these immortal heroes of the faith. He was married (1 Cor. 9:5), but we know nothing beyond the fact of his marriage. His personality stands out in bold outline among the great figures of early Christianity.

CHAPTER V

PHILEMON THE MAN WITH A SOCIAL PROBLEM

There is a peculiar modernness about the problems raised by Paul's Letter to Philemon. Professor Frank Granger showed in the September (1920) *Expositor* that early Christianity faced the chasm between master and slave and sought to bridge it. He rightly insists on the use of the word "slave" for δοῦλος in the New Testament. There has been a curious squeamishness in the use of this word in modern English versions of the New Testament. Professor Granger sees clearly also that Paul's words, addressed to slaves, do not apply in all respects to modern workmen. It is time to make a fresh study of the whole subject.

I. THE LETTER TO PHILEMON NOT AN EPISTLE

Deissmann is right in contending that "Paul's letter to Philemon is no doubt the one most clearly seen to be a letter. Only the colour-blindness of pedantry could possibly regard this delightful little letter as a treatise 'On the Attitude of Christianity to Slavery.' In its intercession for a runaway slave it is exactly parallel to the letter, quoted above (pp. 205-6), from the Papas of Hermupolis to the officer Abinnæus. Read and interpreted as a letter this unobtrusive relic from the age of the first witnesses is one of the most valuable self-revelations that the great apostle has left us: brotherly feeling, quiet beauty, tact as a man of the world—all these are discoverable in the letter" ("Light from the Ancient East," p. 226). It cannot be admitted that Paul's other writings are "letters" in the same sense that Deissmann shows to be true of the one to Philemon. "The letters of Paul are not literary; they are real letters, not epistles; they were written by Paul not for the public and posterity, but for the persons to whom they are addressed. Almost all the mistakes that have ever been made in the study of St. Paul's life and work have arisen from the neglect of the fact that his writings are non-literary and letter-like in character" (*ibid.* p. 225). And Deissmann has made another mistake in trying to make all of Paul's epistles to be of the same mould. We do not have to think that Paul was thinking of posterity. He certainly was not posing. He wrote to meet immediate need by applying the principle of Christianity to actual problems in specific cases. But he wrote for the public beyond a doubt. He wrote for churches or for groups of churches and expected his epistles to be read in public and to be passed on from church to church (Col. 4:16). He gave instructions for testing the genuineness of his epistles (2 Thess. 2:2; 3:17). He expected his commands in his epistles to be obeyed (2 Thess. 3:14). And even the Letter to Philemon includes a message to Apphia, to Archippus, and to the church in his house. Paul makes his appeal to Philemon, but he has in mind in the background the group of disciples who met in the hospitable home of Philemon. It is an utter under-estimate of Paul's epistles to treat them as merely personal and casual. Paul took them seriously and meant them to be received as earnest attempts to in-fluence the lives of the readers. But to Philemon Paul did write a distinctly personal letter about a domestic and social problem, not concerning ecclesiastical or doc-trinal issues as in the Epistles to Timothy and Titus.

It is true, then, that the Letter to Philemon is not a formal Epistle like that to the Church at Rome, nor is it a treatise on the attitude of Christianity to slavery, though the treatment of slavery by Christianity is in-volved, for Paul writes with this very fact in mind. There is this difference, therefore, between Paul's Let-ter to Philemon and the little letter of Caor, Papas of Hermupolis, to Flavius Abinnæus, A.D. 346, concern-ing a runaway soldier by the name of Paul: "I would have thee know, lord, concerning Paul the soldier, concerning his flight: pardon him this once, seeing that I am without leisure to come unto thee at this pres-ent. And, if he desist not, he will come again into thy hands another time."

"This little letter is one of the finest among the papyri," Deissmann adds (p. 205). The situation does in a way resemble the case of Onesimus, though "the Papas is not fit to hold a candle to St. Paul."

The chief reason is that Caor is merely pleasant and playful and makes no effort to grapple with the real issue involved in the soldier's desertion.

Much more pertinent is the letter to a friend by the younger Pliny (Pliny, *Ep.* ix. 21), in which this "no-blest type of a true Roman gentleman" (Lightfoot,

"Commentary," p. 317) in purest diction pleads for pity on the grounds of common humanity. "Your freed-man, with whom you had told me you were vexed, came to me, and throwing himself down before me clung to my feet, as if they had been yours. He was profuse in his tears and his entreaties; he was profuse also in his silence. In short, he convinced me of his penitence. I believe that he is a reformed character, because he feels that he has done wrong. You are angry, I know; and you have reason to be angry, this also I know; but mercy wins the highest praise just when there is the most righteous cause for anger. You loved the man, and, I hope, will continue to love him, meanwhile it is enough that you should allow yourself to yield to his prayers." So Pliny proceeds to plead for his youth, for his tears, for a spirit of gentleness, for a second chance. There is no need to depreciate the nobility of Pliny's plea. Only we must note how unusual this note of pity for the slave is in the Roman world. Pliny passes Paul in the graces of rhetoric, but Paul's spirit strikes deep into the heart of this open sore of the world and searches for the only real cure for the case of Onesimus and for all slaves.

II. THE VALUE OF THE LETTER TO PHILEMON

Lightfoot claims that "as an expression of simple dignity, of refined courtesy, of large sympathy, and of warm personal affection the Epistle to Philemon stands unrivalled" ("Commentary," p. 317). But this high estimate of the letter has not always been held. In the fourth century there was considerable depreciation of the letter on the ground that it was unworthy of Paul to write about a runaway slave. These critics, concerned chiefly about Christological theories, denied that Paul wrote the letter, since it concerned neither doctrine nor ecclesiastical problems. "Of what account was the fate of a single insignificant slave, long since dead and gone, to those before whose eyes the battle of the creeds was still raging?" (Lightfoot). Even Marcion had retained it in his canon and Baur in the last century praised the noble Christian spirit of the letter, while denying that Paul wrote it. But the hyperorthodox critics of the fourth century, like the radical Baur in the nineteenth, were wrong. Jerome, Chrysostom, and Theodore of Mopsuestia ably championed the genuineness of the Letter to Philemon. The arguments that they produced have never been answered. The failure to appreciate the issue at stake in the case of Onesimus is precisely what has made so many nominal Christians ineffective. It is more concern for creed than for conduct, the failure to apply Christianity to the actual conditions of life. Modern Christian scholars, with the exception of Baur and Van Manen, have seen the spirit of Christ in Paul's plea for Onesimus. Luther terms it a "right noble and lovely example of Christian love." Calvin speaks of the "life-like portrayal of the gentleness" of Paul's spirit as seen here. Franke says that "the single Epistle to Philemon very far surpasses all the wisdom of the world." Ewald notes the commanding spirit and tender friendship of Paul "in this letter, at once so brief, and yet so surpassingly full and significant." Sabatier glows with enthusiasm. "We have here only

a few familiar lines, but so full of grace, of salt, of
serious and trustful affection, that this short epistle
gleams like a pearl of the most exquisite purity in the
rich treasure of the New Testament." It is needless
to quote other writers, though Renan calls it "a verit-
able little masterpiece of the art of letter-writing."
We may admit that Paul wrote many personal letters
like this that breathe the spirit of Christ. Some of
them may yet be found. But we can at least be grateful that the Letter to Philemon has been preserved,
that it still carries the message of Christ to the modern
world which is in the throes of a social revolution
that will never be settled till it is settled right, in harmony with the teaching of this little letter.

III.   THE DATE OF THE LETTER

It is certain that Paul was a prisoner at the time
when he wrote, for he speaks of himself as "Paul the
aged, and now a prisoner also of Christ Jesus" (verse
9). The word *presbutes* apparently here means "aged"
and not "ambassador." A number of scholars (Reuss,
Weiss, Hilgenfeld, Holtzmann, Hausrath, Meyer)
have argued for Cæsarea rather than Rome as the
place. Some even contend for Ephesus. But it is
clear that the latter was sent at the same time as that
to Colossæ, since Onesimus (Philemon 10, 13; Col.
4:9) is the bearer of both along with Tychicus who
is also bearer of the Epistle to the Ephesians or Lao-
diceans (Col. 4:7, 16; Eph. 6:21). The arguments
in favour of Cæsarea are quite indecisive. The near-
ness of Cæsarea to Colossæ is really an objection,
since Onesimus could hide in Rome better than in

Cæsarea. The plan of Paul for going to Macedonia (Phil. 2:24) does not weigh against Rome, since Paul could go on to Colossæ from Philippi or the reverse. It is not necessary to decide whether Philippians precedes or follows Philemon, though Philippians probably comes first. At any rate all four epistles come within the period of Paul's first Roman imprisonment (A. D. 60-3). If Paul was born about the beginning of the century, he would be about sixty years old. But he had endured almost incredible hardships and persecutions (2 Cor. 11) that probably made him show his age in a marked degree. Certain it is that he writes as one thoroughly familiar with conditions in the Roman Empire. He writes out of a full heart from the centre of Roman life to a city in a far distant province, but the subject of slavery touches one of the nerve centres of Roman life.

IV. THE PICTURE OF PHILEMON

We know nothing of Philemon except what this letter tells us. The Apostolical Constitutions represent him as bishop of Colossæ and pseudo-Dositheus (sixth century) as bishop of Gaza. Greek Martyrology tells that he, Apphia, Archippus, and Onesimus were all stoned before Androcles the governor in the days of Nero. The Latin Martyrology likewise agrees with this story. In the *Menea* for November 22 he is called a "holy apostle." But all this may be passed by as legendary. Philemon was a citizen of Colossæ (Col. 4:9; Philemon 11). He was a convert of Paul: "Thou owest to me even thine own self besides" (Philemon 19). It is probable, therefore, since Paul had

not been to Colossæ (Col. 2:1), that Philemon was
converted in Ephesus during Paul's three years there
when the gospel spread over the province of Asia (Acts
19:10).   There was easy and constant communication between Ephesus and the Lycus Valley by one of
the Roman roads that linked the great cities together.
It is not certain that Philemon was a preacher.   He
may have been simply an active layman.   Paul speaks
of him as "our beloved and fellow-worker" (Philemon 1), but *sunergos* can apply to a layman.   He had
a church in his house (Philemon 2), though here
again we cannot tell whether it is the whole Church
in Colossæ that met with Philemon because he was
the elder (or one of the elders) or merely a church
group that met in his house for convenience.   In
either case it is plain that Philemon was a man of
some property and standing to afford a house large
enough for this purpose.   Besides, he had slaves, of
whom Onesimus had been one, and a family.   It seems
that Apphia was his wife, and Archippus their son.
Paul speaks affectionately of her as "our sister," and
of Archippus as "our fellow-soldier."   It is suggested
by Zahn that he was the reader of the church, and by
Abbott ("Int. Crit. Comm.") that he was a presbyter
in the Church or at least an evangelist.   It is even
held from Colossians 4:17 that Archippus was elder in
the Church of Laodicea: "And say to Archippus, take
heed to the ministry which thou hast received in the
Lord, that thou fulfil it."   At any rate we have the
picture of a delightful Christian home, where all were
active in Christian service.

As to Philemon Paul has the kindest words of praise

(Philemon 4-7) for him. Paul offers for him one of
the great prayers of all time. This prayer for Philemon follows the usual order, but it is full of passion
and power. He makes mention of Philemon in his
prayers and he is always grateful because of what he
has heard, probably through Epaphras (Col. 1 :7, 8; 4:
12), concerning the love which he had for all the
saints and the faith which he had toward the Lord
Jesus. And yet Paul has "love and faith" together as
if both of them were exercised toward the Lord Jesus
and towards the saints. Certainly both words can
be so employed, though not with quite the same content. First come love for and faith in the Lord Jesus,
then love for and faith in the saints. Paul had experi-
enced (*eschon,* effective aorist) much joy and consolation in the love of Philemon, "because the hearts of
the saints have been refreshed (same verb in Matt. 11:
28, "I will give you rest") through thee, brother"
(Philemon 7). Philemon evidently was liberal and
active in his beneficence, just the sort of man to cheer
a preacher's heart. He was on the look out for opportunities of doing good. So then (ver. 6) Paul prays
"that the fellowship of thy faith may become effectual
in the knowledge of every good thing which is in you,
unto Christ." The fellowship (*koinonia*) is the common word for contribution or more exactly partnership. The word for "effectual" (*energes*) is our word
energy (at work). Paul's prayer, therefore, is that
Philemon's generosity may become really effective,
that he may know it himself, that God may carry him
on in service for Christ. The prayer itself is a tribute

and shows that Paul considers him worthy of the
great things that he means to ask of him.

Paul has a genuine affection for Philemon, as is,
manifest. He is "our beloved and fellow-worker"
(2); he speaks of "thy goodness" (14); "if then thou
countest me partner" (17, *koinonon,* like our "pal"; *cf.*
Luke 5:10. James and John were "partners with
Simon"); "I hope that through your prayers I shall
be granted unto you" (Philemon 22). Paul plainly
feels a close bond of fellowship with Philemon. In all
probability Philemon had come to be one of his chief
helpers in Asia while Paul was in Ephesus. He is thus
at liberty to address Philemon upon any topic.

v. THE CONDUCT OF ONESIMUS

It had been very bad. In plain English, he was a
runaway slave and a thief besides. Paul would hardly
have said, "But if he hath wronged thee at all or oweth
thee aught" (ver. 18), unless it were true. Paul states
the matter delicately and *hypothetically* as a debt, but
his meaning is clear. Onesimus was, of course, still a
heathen when he ran away and defrauded his master
of his services. He may, indeed, have seen Paul in
Ephesus on a visit with his master Philemon, but it
seems clear that he was not converted till coming to
Rome. Evil men, Tacitus says, flocked to Rome,
gladiators, soldiers, soothsayers, slaves. Among the
Jews slaves were very few, but in Athens there were
four times as many slaves as citizens. Wealthy Roman
landowners sometimes possessed twenty thousand
slaves. It is not known how many slaves were in the
Roman Empire, probably six or seven million. These

slaves were sometimes very degraded people, sometimes people of culture and former wealth, victims of
war and rapine. Freedmen like Epictetus often represented the highest culture of the community and were
the school-teachers and philosophers of the time.
Roman law gave the slave no rights and no protection.
Not till Constantine's time did they have any rights
as husband and wife. Even Aristotle spoke of the
slave as a "live chattel" or property (*Pol.* i, 4) or a
"live implement" (*Eth. Nic.* viii, 13). "The slave was
absolutely at his master's disposal; for the smallest
offence he might be scourged, mutilated, crucified,
thrown to the wild beasts" (Lightfoot, p. 319). A
Roman senator, Pedanius Secundus, had been slain by
one of his slaves in anger. In revenge four hundred
slaves were executed. The populace rebelled and tried
to prevent the tragedy, but Roman soldiers lined the
road as the slaves were led to execution. Rome lived
over a volcano and each man had "as many enemies as
slaves." Onesimus was not merely a runaway slave
and a thief, a representative of "the least respectable
type of the least respectable class in the social scale"
(Lightfoot, p. 309), but he was also a Phrygian slave.
The Phrygians were despised most of all, and Onesimus had lived up to the bad reputation of his race
and of his class. His name, forsooth, was good enough
(meaning "useful") but he had proved "unprofitable"
(Philemon 11) to Philemon. Paul makes the pun upon
his name after his conversion when he had proved true
to his name. Many slaves and freedmen bore the
name Onesimus. Paul does not try to conceal the
crime of Onesimus. He had sunk to the bottom.

He had come to Rome and wallowed in this cesspool
of humanity as one of the offscourings of humanity.
He was in no sense a hero, not even with Paul. One
is reminded of the "underground railway" before and
during the Civil War in the United States, when the
runaway slaves escaped over the Ohio River to freedom. It is a dark picture even as Paul draws it with
his delicate and sympathetic pen.

VI. THE PROBLEM BEFORE PAUL

We do not know why Onesimus came to Paul, who
was himself a prisoner under military guard, though
living in his own hired house. It may have been
Epaphras who recognised Onesimus and who brought
him to Paul. It may have been one of the soldiers
whom Paul had won to Christ. It may have been the
memory of the words of Philemon or of others at the
gatherings in Colossæ; it may have been the lashings
of a guilty conscience; it may have been sheer want
from hunger or even desperation (Lightfoot). Of
this we cannot tell. The famous Rescue Mission
worker, Rev. Melvin Trotter, was on the way to commit suicide in Lake Michigan, when he was drawn into
the Pacific Garden Mission in Chicago and converted.
The hour of man's extremity is God's opportunity.
Somehow Onesimus came under the spell of Paul's
influence and was won to Christ. The conversion was
genuine and Paul was sure of the result. But what
should Paul advise Onesimus to do? Legally he was
still the slave of Philemon, who could put him to death
for his crime. Certainly Philemon, as a Christian,
would not do that. But should Onesimus go back at

all and re-enter the life of slavery now that he was
Christ's freeman? The answer is not an easy one.
"Onesimus had repented, but he had not made restitution" (Lightfoot). D. L. Moody used to preach the
duty of restitution with great vigour. Onesimus could
not offer to make restitution without going back under
the yoke of slavery. Shall Paul send him back? That
is the problem. If he does not send him back he has
wronged both Onesimus and Philemon. If he sends
him back he may likewise wrong them both if Philemon continues to treat Onesimus merely as a slave as
if nothing had changed their relations with each other.
So Paul chooses the latter alternative. He will send
Onesimus back to Philemon under the guard of Tychicus (Col. 4:7-9), but with a powerful appeal to
Philemon for forgiveness towards Onesimus. Did he
do right? Should he have done more? Should he
have attacked slavery as an institution? Should he
have aroused the slaves in the Roman Empire to re-
volt? Did Paul wink at slavery?

VII.   PAUL'S PLEA FOR ONESIMUS

It is not admitted by all that Paul recognised slavery
to be an evil. He does urge Christian slaves to be
indifferent to their bondage (1 Cor. 7:21), "but if
thou canst become free, use it rather" (margin of Re-
vised Version), that is, "become free." Certainly Paul
means (7:22f.) that our relation to Christ is the main
thing. The slave can be Christ's freedman. That is
the chief thing. But Paul taught the Christian doctrine of liberty that works against all autocracy and
oppression: "There can be neither Jew nor Greek,

there can be neither bond nor free, there can be no male and female; for ye are all one man in Christ Jesus" (Gal. 3:28). That is absolutely revolutionary doctrine, as I have tried to show in my book, "The New Citizenship." That leaven began to work in the first century as the result of Paul's preaching. "The old world was parted by deep gulfs. There were three of special depth and width, across which it was hard for sympathy to fly. These were the distinctions of race, sex, and condition" (Maclaren, "Colossians and Philemon," p. 224). We do not have to say that Paul thought out the full development of this platform of freedom. The important thing is that he had proclaimed it. He had urged Christian slaves to be good servants, but he had insisted that Christian masters be just and merciful to their slaves. Paul was not unconcerned about the social wrongs in the world of his day. He attacked those wrongs courageously and with consummate wisdom.

In the letter to Philemon Paul applies his principle of freedom in Christ to the specific case of Onesimus. He is in the realm of the concrete, and is not a mere doctrinaire reformer. It is to be noted at once that Paul deals with Onesimus as a man and as a brother. There were occasional instances of pity for slaves on the part of masters, as in the case of the younger Pliny (Ep. 8:16), but as a rule there was an utter lack of regard for the slave as a man at all. Aristotle thought that one should have no friendship with a slave as a slave, but might deal with him as a man. No such subtle philosophy troubled Paul. Paul took Onesimus "both in the flesh and in the Lord" (Philemon 16), "as a brother beloved" (16), as his very "child" (10), as Paul's "very heart" (12). We know from the papyri that many slaves became Christians. The Letter to Philemon makes it plain why it was true. Here alone, in Christianity, were slaves treated as human beings. Here they were called "brothers." Here they could find usefulness and promotion. Many of the slaves became pastors of the Churches. The millions of slaves in the Roman Empire saw in Christianity their one ray of hope. They were right. Christianity is still fighting the battles of race, class, and sex. The great war that is just over gathered up all these issues. They will be fought to a finish in accord with the Spirit of Christ.

Paul does not leave the case there. He does unhesitatingly and frankly take Onesimus to his bosom and heart as a brother in Christ. But he does more. He boldly asks that Philemon shall do the same. But not without restitution. Paul gives his note of hand to that effect. "I will repay it" (ver. 19). "Put that to mine account" (ver. 18). Paul uses the technical language for debt that is so common in the papyri. But that is merely to clear the path for the real test. Paul asks that Philemon take Onesimus back, without punishment, to be sure. Paul has sent him back reluctantly because he had found him useful (vers. 12f.). But he wishes Philemon to have the privilege of being generous with Onesimus (vers. 14f.). Paul claims the right as an apostle to enjoin (give military orders, *epitassein*, ver. 8) upon Philemon what is befitting. Moral propriety (*cf.* Col. 3:18, for this same word) brings moral obligation. Paul wishes Philemon to have the chance to come up of his own accord, willingly and as a matter of judgment, not of necessity under pressure from Paul (Philemon 14). Hence Paul appeals and exhorts by reason of love as the true principle by which to act. He adds also the fact that Paul who pleads for Onesimus is the aged (or the ambassador of Jesus) and a prisoner of Christ, and has a right to be heard by reason of the scars of service that he bears (*cf.* Gal. 6:17).

Paul does not wish Philemon to think that he is trying to push off on him a tough case that is in his way. On the contrary, he has found positive pleasure in the service of Onesimus, and could wish to keep him both for his own worth and to take the place of Philemon who is so far away (vers. 12, 13). It is a delicate compliment to both Philemon and Onesimus. The essential refinement of Paul's nature appears at every turn in this charming and courteous and ennobling letter. Paul appeals to the best side of Philemon's nature. He assumes that his being a slaveholder had not debased his humanitarian feelings. The tendency was in that direction, as "Uncle Tom's Cabin" showed. But it was not necessary for a Christian man to yield to the brutalising influence of mere power, as the lives of Washington, Lee, and Jackson abundantly prove. The nobler side of the institution of slavery in the South is well shown in Mrs. Smede's "The Southern Planter" and in Thomas Nelson Page's "Marse Chan" and other Virginian stories. But the peril of slavery was and is that the slave was at the mercy of a conscienceless master who could hold him down and even ruin his life.

Paul treats with Philemon on the basis of humanity and Christianity. He admits all the technical legal claims upon Onesimus, but boldly begs for his reception by Philemon not merely as a pardoned runaway slave who is restored to his former status. That is only the first step. Paul dares to go further and to ask that Philemon receive him "no longer as a slave, but more than a slave, a brother beloved, specially to me, but how much rather to thee, both in the flesh and in the Lord" (ver. 16). Imagine a slave in the home who is no longer a slave, but a brother beloved! It is a revolutionary request, possible only on the plea of love. "For perhaps he was therefore parted *from thee* for a season, that thou shouldest have him for ever" (ver. 15). Could anything surpass this turn in interpreting God's overruling providence?

Paul is fully aware that he has gone pretty far with Philemon. But he means to go farther. "If then thou countest me a partner, receive him as myself" (ver. 17). He expects Onesimus to be treated in all essentials as Paul would be in social and religious privileges. It is clear that Onesimus was a man of parts in spite of his conduct and his Phrygian blood. There was the making of a man in him. Paul wants him to have his chance. He is expecting to come to see Philemon when, through his prayers, he is released from bondage in Rome, and he confidently asks that his lodging be gotten ready (ver. 22). All this adds to the piquancy of the request for handsome treatment of Onesimus, as if Paul had already come. It is the perfection of courtesy and dignity and courage. Paul is sure that Philemon wishes to make him happy: "Yea, brother, let me have joy of thee in the Lord: refresh my heart in Christ" (ver. 20). The very word for "have joy" (*onaimēn*) is the same root as the name Onesimus, itself a playful plea for the Christian slave. The word for "refresh" is the one already employed concerning Philemon in verse 7. The word for "heart" is here the third time in the letter (7, 12, 20), and is a very tender emotional word of strong feeling.

Surely St. Paul has finished his plea. But no, he has one more word before he closes. It is plain enough that, if Philemon accedes to Paul's request, Onesimus will be "no longer a slave." He must be set free. And yet Paul hesitates to write that word. He means it, and he makes Philemon see it staring at him all through the letter, but he wishes Philemon to spell it voluntarily, "that thy goodness should not be as of necessity, but of free will" (ver. 14). Freedmen were common enough in the Roman Empire. Sometimes freedom was won by some deed of heroism. The slave occasionally saved money and bought his own freedom. The master sometimes voluntarily freed a slave. Sometimes a man of generous impulses paid the price of a slave and set him free. The papyri and ostraca furnish many illustrations of Paul's very language on this point (Gal. 5:1, 13). Christ paid the price of our bondage with His blood and set us free. This is the language of Paul and Peter and of John. "For freedom did Christ set us free" (Gal. 5:1). Paul will not use the word "freedom" to Philemon, but he ventures to hint it so clearly that there can be no mistake. "Having confidence in thine obedience, I write unto thee, knowing that thou wilt do even beyond what I say" (ver.

21). Beyond what Paul had said, but not beyond what he had meant. Paul is sure that the sense of duty in Philemon will compel obedience to the highest things. *Noblesse oblige.* The very nobility of Philemon's character as a Christian will compel him to set Onesimus free. So Paul rests his plea. The word for freedom has trembled on his lips all through the letter, but out of considerations of respect for Philemon it has not escaped. But Philemon was bound to know what Paul meant.

Did he set Onesimus free? We do not know. "It cannot be imagined that this appeal in behalf of Onesimus was in vain" (Rutherford). Tradition ("Apostolical Canons," 82) relates that Philemon forgave Onesimus and manumitted him. All sorts of rumours gained currency about Onesimus. One is that he became bishop in Berœa ("Apost. Const." vii, 46), another that he journeyed to Spain, another that he was martyred in Rome or at Puteoli. E. A. Abbott has written a fictitious story of what might have happened to him in his "Onesimus."

VIII. CHRISTIANITY IN THE MARKET PLACE

Why did not Paul attack slavery as an institution? Did he mean to imply that slavery is wrong *per se?* These questions are easier to ask than to answer. Advocates of slavery have claimed that Paul in the Letter to Philemon condones slavery as an institution. Enemies of slavery argue that he shows himself the foe of slavery. Vincent ("Int. Crit. Comm.," p. 165) thinks that "it is more than questionable whether St. Paul had grasped the postulate of the modern Chris-

tian consciousness that no man has the right to own
another." It was not necessary for him to see that.
But Paul was bound to be conscious of what he was
doing. He definitely and boldly took the side of liberty
in this plea for Onesimus as he had fought for and
had won the freedom of Titus from Jewish legalism
(Gal. 2:1-10). The whole issue was summed up in
each instance in a concrete case. "The letter to Philemon is the first indication in Christian literature that
the problem of the relation of master to slave must be
seriously affected by the new conception of the brotherhood of man, which Christ's apostles had set themselves
to proclaim" (Bernard). A little leaven would in time
leaven the whole lump. It seems a long step and a
long time from Paul's gracious words to Philemon to
Lincoln's blunt assertion that the Union cannot continue half-slave and half-free. But it is safe to affirm
that Paul made possible Lincoln's emancipation proclamation.

Paul was not an anarchist, as is plain from Romans
13:1-7. He believed in government, and taught
obedience save where conscience was attacked. Then
he was not slow to assert his rights. The slave was
quick to see the help that Christianity offered him. The
slaves flocked to Christ in large numbers. Christianity
had to show that its adherents could make good citizens
of the Roman Empire as well as good members of the
kingdom of heaven. That issue is still a vital one.
Christ and Cæsar are still rival claimants for our
loyalty. Some men have not learned how to be true
to both. "Whatever may have been the range of Paul's
outlook, the policy which he pursued vindicated itself

in the subsequent history of slavery. The principles of the gospel not only curtailed its abuses, but destroyed the thing itself; for it could not exist without its abuses" (Vincent, p. 167). Paul insisted on the duty of the master to be just to the slave (Eph. 6:9; Col. 4:1). Christians learned the habit of freeing their slaves. "Sepulchral paintings often represent the master standing before the Good Shepherd with a band of slaves liberated at his death, pleading for him at the last judgment" (Vincent, p. 168). Christian slaves sat side by side with the master in church and partook of the communion together. Slaves became presbyters. "The Christian teachers and clergymen became known as 'the brothers of the slave,' and the slaves themselves were called 'the freedmen of Christ'" (Brace, "Gesta Christi"). From Constantine to the tenth century laws were passed to help the slaves.

One may grow impatient that it took so long for the shackles to be loosed from the slaves of the world even in so-called Christian lands. One has to reckon with the grip of money and selfishness and love of power and pleasure. Even Christian men relax their hold upon privilege and power slowly and reluctantly. But the principle of love and equality in the Letter to Philemon was in the end bound to destroy slavery. "It was only a question of time" (Lightfoot).

There have been times when Christianity was called a dead letter because slavery was allowed. It has even been justified by Christian preachers. But the chivalry of the gospel was at work. Social prejudices received a wound when slave girls like Blandina in Gaul or Felicitas in Africa became martyrs and were celebrated in festivals (Lightfoot). The day came when Britain turned upon slavery as an accursed thing. "The abolition of slavery throughout the British Empire at an enormous material sacrifice is one of the greatest moral conquests which England has ever achieved" (Lightfoot, pp. 326f.). In the United States we were not so wise, and it cost blood and treasure untold to set the negro free. But it was done in Britain and America in response to the Christian impulse. Lightfoot dares to claim that the era of liberation for mankind came as a result of the Letter to Philemon. The leaven had finally done its work.

But all men are not yet free. The gospel of liberty must still be proclaimed on the housetop and in the market-place. Paul met the philosophers in the market-place at Athens. He did not hesitate to come to close grips with them. He likewise joined issue with human greed and love of power over other men in the case of Onesimus. He did not shrink from the issue, and squarely put the matter up to Philemon. Paul was a mystic and a transcendentalist. He taught other-worldliness as a blessed hope, as the mainstay of the life that now is. But Paul was a practical idealist. He had no patience with putting up with ills that could be cured. There were plenty to endure that were beyond relief. Paul was a social reformer who cut at the root of current abuses. He did not try to tear down the whole structure of human society at one blow. He preached principles that would inevitably make a heaven out of earth if men had the courage to put them into practice. He did not preach a kingdom of heaven that concerned only the future life. His real citizenship was in heaven even while on earth, but this conception involved living on earth like a citizen of heaven—member of a colony of heaven on earth.

In the end slavery has gone down in response to Paul's interpretation of the gospel of Christ. The grip of alcohol is likewise now loosened. America has gone ahead of Britain in the abolition of this slavery of the soul and body. Sex prejudice is slowly giving way, more rapidly in Britain than in America. Race prejudice is still alive in spite of the League of Nations. The great war has not slain this dragon that is already again raising his head over the world.

But Christianity cannot shirk the issue. It is in the market-place. It is in the midst of the fight to rescue men like Onesimus who have become the victims of human greed, to set women free from man's lust, to give children a chance to grow into the full stature of manhood in Christ Jesus. The Letter to Philemon is the *Magna Charta* of the human spirit. The only real freedom is that in Christ. When the Son sets us free, we are free in reality, free to do right to other men, free to fight the cause of liberty for all nations, for all classes, for both sexes. The foes of freedom are not dead, but liberty is winning its way. The star of democracy is in the ascendant, and the star of autocracy is at last going down in defeat. The world cannot always continue half-slave and half-free.

CHAPTER VI

STEPHEN THE PATHBREAKER AND THE MARTYR

I. AN EPOCH-MARKING MAN

Stephen does not cut a very large figure in the book of Acts. His story comes wholly in chapters 6 and 7, save Paul's allusion to him in 22:20 as "Stephen thy witness" (martyr), "but its vital importance for the history is obvious from the pages of the Acts" (Rackham).

He stands at the parting of the ways and marks a revolution within Jewish Christianity. His speech is the longest in the Acts and Luke evidently regarded him as the true transition from Peter to Paul. He was a "new man" (Rackham) and so well suited to an era of reconstruction. He was a pioneer of progress and, as is often the case, paid the penalty for his prophetic insight and foresight by being ahead of his age. We need not say that he created the crisis between Christianity and Judaism, for that was inevitable. But he precipitated it and so challenges our interest to-day.

II. A MAN OF RARE GIFTS FOR THE EMERGENCY

He comes into the story in a rather incidental way as one of the Seven who were chosen to "serve tables" ($\delta\iota\alpha\kappa\sigma\nu\epsilon\hat{\iota}\nu$ $\tau\rho\alpha\pi\epsilon\zeta\alpha\iota\varsigma$, Acts 6:2) so that the twelve might devote themselves to prayer and to the ministry of the word" (τῇ διακονία τοῦ λόγου, verse 4). The distribution of the funds for the poor (chaps. 3 and 4) had taken too much of the time of the apostles who had to "leave the word" (6:2) "to minister to tables."

The modern minister is constantly exposed to this very temptation. He must be a church, denominational, and civic leader. The merely administrative side of his task threatens to thrust the spiritual and educational to one side. Paul carried the balance well as missionary, statesman, evangelist, teacher, theologian, author, pastor.

Perhaps the twelve might not have felt the burden so keenly but for the criticism of the Hellenistic (Greek-speaking Jews from without Palestine) Christians that the Hellenistic widows were discriminated against in the distribution of the common funds. One of the largest givers was Barnabas, Hellenist, of Cyprus. It is not easy to allay suspicion of that nature, however unjust. The twelve adopted the bold plan of asking the church to choose seven men, approved by the church, full of the Holy Spirit and wisdom, men whom the whole church trusted.

It was a wise solution of the predicament. It seems likely, though not certain, that "deacons" grew out of this arrangement. There is no mention of "elders" till Acts 11:30. Besides, all (or nearly all, if we judge by their names) of the Seven were Hellenists. Thus the Hellenists must now judge the fairness of a Hellenistic body, not of an Aramæan body like the Twelve.

First of the Seven

The outstanding man in the list of seven is Stephen. Crown ($\sigma\tau\acute{\epsilon}\varphi\alpha\nu\text{os}$) is the meaning of his name. He won the martyr's crown and wore the halo of glory from the face of Christ. He heads the list as "a man full of faith and of the Holy Spirit" (6:5). He entered upon his work "full of grace and power" who also "wrought great wonders and signs among the people" (6:8).

It is plain that Stephen was like Paul in the combination of the mystic and the practical. He was a man of vision who brought things to pass. He was a poet in both senses of the word (the seer and the doer). He had faith and grace (trust and charm). He had wisdom and power. Without faith one cannot pierce the veil of the future. Without grace he cannot win followers. Without wisdom he cannot lucidly project his vision into the realm of the practical. Without power (dynamite, $\delta\acute{\upsilon}\nu\sigma\alpha\mu\iota s$) he cannot drive it through to realisation. Stephen had all these powers and energies and the gift of the Holy Spirit who suffered with divine afflatus all that he did. He was a combination of the practical idealism of Woodrow Wilson, the hardheadedness of Clemenceau, and the dynamic energy of Lloyd George. "We have the story of but one day in his life, the last: yet there is no man in the New Testament of whom we are told so much without one blemish being revealed" (Furneaux).

Stephen furnishes one of the famous "ifs" of history. If he had lived, who can tell what his career would have been? Would he have challenged first place with Paul as the heroic pathfinder for Christianity? Already he excelled the twelve in his philosophic grasp of the significance of the Christian movement in its bearing on Judaism.

Stephen belongs to the long list of gifted young men cut off in the prime of power and promise like Keats, like Rupert Brooke and many another genius sacrificed in the plenitude of hope. Stephen wrought miracles and had every mark of the seal of the Holy Spirit upon his work.

III. AN IRRESISTIBLE APOLOGIST FOR THE FAITH

He cut a wide swath among the people and soon swept beyond the office for which he was chosen.

If Stephen and Philip (the evangelist, as he became) are types for modern deacons, some of them fall far short of their opportunities. The average deacon takes this office more as an honour than as a call to service. It must be remembered that all the early disciples are witnesses for Christ. One of the saddest misfortunes in Christian history is the officialism that has confined soul-winning so largely to preachers, some of whom do not know how to do that, but only to deliver sermons.

Certainly Stephen did not feel that being one of the Seven cut him out of preaching the Word. The rather it gave him a fresh prominence and a new leadership among the Hellenists whose representative he was. So we see this deacon and lay-preacher busy in the Hellenistic synagogues of Jerusalem.

His bold and powerful proclamation of the gospel

of grace and freedom in Christ awakened opposition in these synagogues. Stephen became the centre of debate as the champions of Judaism challenged his presentation of Christianity and Judaism, "disputing with Stephen" (συνζητοῦντες τῷ Στεφάνῳ).

It was exciting work, we may be sure, but Stephen was flushed with victory, for "they were not able to resist the wisdom and the Spirit with which he spoke" 6:10). They rose up quickly (ἀνέστησαν, aorist tense, ingressive action), but they had not strength to stand against (οὐκ ἴσχυονἀντιστῆναι) this spiritual tornado that swept down all in his path.

A New Type of Preacher

For the moment Stephen, not Peter, held the centre of the stage in Jerusalem. Stephen was a new type of preacher. He had Hellenic culture, was possibly an Alexandrian, and was able, like Apollos and Paul after him, to give a philosophic interpretation of Christianity that was out of Peter's range.

There is no evidence that the twelve felt any jealousy of Stephen nor was there opportunity for them to come to his help at his trial. They themselves had been on trial before the same Sanhedrin.

Stephen undoubtedly alarmed the rabbis by the power of his message. Their very failure to answer "this first great apologist for Christianity" (Press, Int. St. "Bible Encyclopædia") reminded them of Jesus in the Temple whose destruction he foretold on Olivet. Stephen dared to proclaim the perfect equality of Jew and Gentile in the Kingdom of God and he showed the spiritual nature of worship as Jesus had done to the woman at the well (John 4).

Among those rabbis who rallied to the defence of Jewish orthodoxy was probably the young man Saul, the pride of Gamaliel and his school. In the Cilician synagogue this brilliant young rabbi of Tarsus who had led all his fellow-students in Judaism (Gal. 1:14) met Stephen and, like the rest, fell before the might of Stephen's arguments.

A public humiliation is hard for a proud man to endure. For the moment Christianity was triumphant unless Stephen could be gotten out of the way. The people were with Stephen. Why were the rabbis so opposed to him?

IV. PROPHET OF THE INEVITABLE BREACH BETWEEN CHRISTIANITY AND JUDAISM

It is not every man who can see the drift of a new message or policy. Most people run in ruts until jolted out by a sudden clash. The Pharisees were quick to see that the message of Jesus meant their own undoing if his theory of the Kingdom won the day. They were right in their suspicion toward Jesus as an iconoclast and revolutionist from the standpoint of Pharisaic traditionalism. His emphasis on spiritual reality and moral righteousness made their professional and pietistic functions seem empty and hollow. At bottom the Pharisees killed Jesus for his picture of their own theological and political hopes.

The twelve apostles naturally stressed the fact that the resurrection of Jesus from the dead, and the Sadducees challenged their claim with energy and bitter resentment. Gamaliel and the Pharisees held aloof and apparently enjoyed the predicament of the Sadducees, their hated rivals in the Sanhedrin.

Struck Out on a New Line

But Stephen struck out on a new line and showed how Judaism was preparatory for Christianity and was temporary and would pass away. His Hellenic culture undoubtedly made it easier for Stephen to see the true relation of Judaism and Christianity as was true also with Paul. Peter had a hard struggle to see how Gentiles could be saved without first becoming Jews, though he did see it after Stephen's death (Acts 10 and 11).

But there is enough in the teaching of Jesus to explain all that Stephen said. Jesus had explained about the new patch on the old garment and new wine in old bottles to show that Christianity was a spiritual revolution and was not to be cribbed and cabined by the current Judaism. The worship of God is spiritual whether in Jerusalem or on Mt. Gerizim (John 4:20ff.). Jesus had charged Pharisaism with being hypocritical formalism at variance with the word of God (Mark 7:6) and had predicted the destruction of the temple (Mark 13:2) and the passing of the Kingdom of God to the Gentiles (Matt. 21:43).

The twelve apostles had not as yet seized upon this phase of Christ's teaching. But Stephen boldly proclaimed the spiritual nature of the worship of God irrespective of nation or place. He did it, moreover, with such cogency and clarity that he carried the Hellenists in the synagogue with him. A new force had to be reckoned with and the Pharisees once more sprang to the rescue of the ark of Judaism.

Religious Demagogy

These conscientious inquisitors and persecutors had the zeal of fanatics and were without scruples if so be they could compass their ends. And it must be noted that Hellenists attacked Stephen with the same zeal of the Palestinian or Aramæan Jews. Beaten in debate by Stephen his opponents "suborned men" who were willing to perjure themselves for pay in the interest of Jewish orthodoxy. "We heard him speak blasphemous words against Moses and God." They twisted his interpretation of Christianity in terms of mankind to be a direct attack on Moses who is here mentioned before God. Moses stood for all the Pharisaic theology and they "stirred up the people and the elders and the scribes" by the charge that Stephen was seeking to undermine Judaism.

It is not hard to make an *ad captandum* plea to the populace. Stephen soon found himself under arrest for heresy and arraigned before the Sanhedrin. The mob had rushed at him in their rage and were now ready to believe false witnesses who said, "This fellow does not cease to speak words against this holy place and the law, for we heard him say that Jesus, this Nazarene, will destroy this place and will change the customs that Moses delivered unto us" (Acts 6:13).

It was to their thinking both blasphemy and heresy. In fact, it was neither. Stephen was the true interpreter of Moses as was Jesus. He taught the real worship of God in the spirit. He foresaw the inevitable disappearance of Judaism before Christianity and in a prophetic spirit predicted it. But Stephen did not deny the divine origin of the Mosaic law; he did not revile the temple. But Jewish national pride was aroused against Stephen by the specious charge. Piety and patriotism blazed out at him. What could he say in defence of his attitude?

V. A COURAGEOUS INTERPRETER OF JEWISH HISTORY

It was Stephen's supreme hour. He felt it and was looking unto Jesus for help. We read of none of the disciples who offered sympathy and help at this hour. They may have been cowed into silence. Some may have thought Stephen too bold and aggressive.

But a strange thing happened. The people gazed in awe at the face of Stephen which was transfigured with glory like that of Moses when he came down from the mount when he had been talking with Jehovah.

The young man Saul noticed it and long years afterwards understood what it meant (2 Cor. 3:18). Stephen saw Jesus and the glory of God (Acts 7:55) and his very face shone with the inward peace and light that radiated with a halo, as if his face were that of an angel.

Stephen probably thought rapidly as he recalled the fate of Jesus before this very body on precisely similar charges. He doubtless knew before he spoke what his fate would be. Pilate had surrendered to the Sanhedrin then, and there was small hope that Roman power would intervene in behalf of Stephen now. All that Stephen could do was to speak a clear and true word that would define the issue for which he was to die. Thus he might do much by dying for his Lord and for the freedom of the human spirit.

A Skilful Argument

His apology is really exceedingly skilful and adroit though at first one is surprised that the charges are not directly answered and the name of Jesus does not occur. But his address does answer the charges completely and it is a great and notable defence of Christ. He recounts Jewish history from Abraham to Solomon with philosophic grasp and spiritual insight.

He holds the attention of these rabid Jews as he retells the familiar and wonderful story. But he gives a fresh turn to the narrative that startles while it enthralls them. He shows that the worship of God in one place was not true at the beginning, and was temporary and not essential. He shows how the people had misunderstood God's hand with them and had killed the prophets, who were called to interpret His will to them. Even when the temple came "they made external worship a substitute for spiritual obedience" (Furneaux).

It was a complete justification of Christ and of Stephen's exposition of the gospel. He knew his Old Testament like an Alexandrian theologian and criticised materialistic religion like a Greek, but his idea of redemption and mediation was distinctly Christian (Rackham).

But the breath of the hills did not suit Pharisaism. Stephen saw the flash of anger in the eyes of the members of the Sanhedrin as they saw the drift of his great address which Luke has preserved with wonderful skill. Stephen had not won his judges, though he had won his case and his cause before God and men. What must he now do?

Stephen was not afraid to reveal the Jews to themselves. Jesus had done the same thing in his terrific denunciation of the Pharisees (Matt. 23). They were children of their fathers. They have killed Jesus as they did the prophets before him. He spoke in pity while his words burned the eyes of his hearers like Isaiah's coals of fire.

His keen irony had stung them to the quick. His sarcasm (Acts 7:50-53) cut to the bone (Acts 7:54): "And hearing these things they were sawn asunder (διεπρίοντο) in their hearts, and they began to gnash (ἔβρυχον) their teeth at him. The words of Stephen cut like a buzz-saw and their teeth clattered like wolves for their victim.

They were already murderers at heart. The very truth of the exposition of God's purposes of grace angered them all the more, when at last they saw the point of his speech.

Stephen saw the human wolves leap up at him as he looked up to heaven. He saw the glory of God and Jesus standing at the right hand of God in majesty and glory, standing as if to welcome his faithful witness who has resisted unto blood.

Stephen is rapt with the glory of the vision and cares not for his murderers. He calmly says, "Behold, I see the heavens opened and the Son of man standing at the right hand of God" (Acts 7:56). Jesus saw the

heavens as he came up out of the baptismal waters.
Now the Son of man stands by God's throne to greet
the victor in his death.

It is a glorious transfiguration and intensifies the
rage of the Jews. They lost all restraint. The Sanhedrin became a mob and with loud outcry rushed at
Stephen and hurled him out of the city and began to
stone him (ἐλιθοβόλουν).

A Common Lynching

They were observing some of the forms of Jewish
law at any rate in taking him out of the city and in
stoning him for blasphemy. But all the same it was
murder, a common lynching. No vote of condemnation was taken and the Sanhedrin no longer had the
power of life and death. The Romans were not consulted. The Jews could represent it as an uprising
of the people beyond the control of the Sanhedrin
so that the Romans would let it pass.

Stephen is called "the witness" or martyr of Jesus
and the same word is used of "the witnesses" (οἱ
μάρτυρες, Acts 7:58) who now "laid their clothes
at the feet of a young man named Saul," evidently
the master of ceremonies, who is now having his
revenge on Stephen for defeating him in debate.

These "witnesses" began the stoning as was their
privilege. It was too dirty work for the nice young
rabbi from Tarsus. They pelted Stephen as he gazed
into heaven and said: "Lord Jesus, receive my spirit,"
as if glad to go. Then, bending his knees in spite of
the rocks hurled at him, he prayed to Jesus, "Lord,
lay not this sin to their charge" (Acts 7:60).

He died with forgiveness of his enemies in his heart, this first martyr for Christ, as he sealed with his blood the testimony of his life. Stephen was faithful to the death. Was his witness in vain? It seemed so at the time. But God's plans work slowly, but surely.

VII.   THE FORERUNNER OF PAUL

"And Saul was well-pleased at his death" (Acts 8:1).

There was little of cheer to the Christians in this situation. Besides, Saul at once set about to root out the pestiferous heresy of Christianity from Jerusalem. Like a wolf he ravished the fold and put men and women to death and drove others far afield. The taste for blood grew with the gratification, and Saul, like a war-horse, sniffed the battle as far as Damascus.

The cause of Stephen seemed lost and that of Saul triumphant. The apostles alone were left in Jerusalem, though why we cannot tell. Was it that the friendship of Gamaliel still shielded them from the wrath of Saul, his pupil? Did their failure to come to the rescue of Stephen mollify Saul? Was Saul afraid of the twelve? At any rate the cause of Christ seemed almost annihilated as Saul swept on his victorious career.

And yet, when Jesus checked Saul, he told him that it was hard for him to kick against the goad. Thus we catch a light on these days of vehement victory when Saul fought to drown his own conscience. Stephen had left his mark upon Saul. Stephen, not Gamaliel, was to be the real teacher of Saul.

"Si Stephanus non orasset, ecclesia Paulum non

habuisset." So we may conclude. At any rate Saul, who caused Stephen's death, came to be the real successor of Stephen. Saul took up, expounded, and carried on the teaching of Stephen about the universal message and mission of Christianity. Saul will one day meet the fierce hatred of Jew and Judaiser as he fights for a free gospel for all men. Stephen is vindicated in Paul.

Thus God wrought His will in spite of the wrath of man. Paul himself one day won the martyr's crown (στέφανος). No one, we may be sure, gave Paul a warmer welcome to heaven than Stephen, who could justly claim Paul as his trophy for Christ.

CHAPTER VII

LYDIA THE PREACHER'S FRIEND AND HELPER

There are few characters in the New Testament more attractive than Lydia, of Philippi. Luke has drawn her portrait with wonderful clearness in Acts 16. She is not mentioned elsewhere. A number of points stand out very definitely.

I. A PROGRESSIVE WOMAN OF BUSINESS

There is a curious modernness about Lydia, of Thyatira, seller of purple in Philippi (Acts 16:14).

Strabo calls Thyatira a Mysian town, but Ptolemy locates it in Lydia. It was on the border of Mysia, but in Lydia, and was included by the Romans in the province of Asia. It was a flourishing trade center, though surpassed by Ephesus, Smyrna and Pergamos. It is one of the cities addressed in Revelation (2:18-29). There were numerous guilds like the clothiers, braziers and dyers. Lydia evidently belonged to the guild of dyers in Thyatira as "a seller of purple."

Purple was the color of the official stripe on the Roman togas worn at Rome and in the colonies. Thyatira was chiefly famous for the fine purple cloth manufactured there. The country of Lydia was the richest and most prosperous in Western Asia Minor.

It seems clear that Lydia was a woman of means to

be able to deal in this expensive clothing. The very term "royal purple" is suggested by her business. It is not clear whether Lydia is her real name or merely "the Lydian" to the people of Philippi. Horace employs the name for Roman women and finally at any rate in Philippi she was called Lydia.

She is not mentioned in Paul's Epistle to the Philippians. She may have returned to Thyatira or she may have been dead by then. It is .suggested that Paul refers to her under the name Euodia or Syntyche (Phil. 4:2). Renan has even argued that she was Paul's wife and is addressed in Philippians 4:3, "true yokefellow." But that carries one very far afield in the realm of mere speculation.

Since she had abundant means, it is quite possible that she could have met the expenses of Paul's first trial in Rome unless, as Ramsay thinks, Paul had come into possession of his father's patrimony. We are to think, then, of Lydia at the head of a large establishment that employed many women. (cf. Acts 16:13).

Philippin, like other cities in Macedonia (Berœa, Thessalonica), allowed more freedom to women than they enjoyed in Athens, Corinth or Ephesus (cf. Ramsay, "St. Paul the Traveller and Roman Citizen," pp. 224, 227, 232). Macedonian inscriptions show that women enjoyed higher social·position and considerable freedom. In Thessalonica (modern Saloniki) Paul won "of the chief women not a few" (Acts 17:4) and in Berœa many "of the Greek women of honourable estate" (Acts 17:12). It is quite appropriate therefore, now that women have won citizenship in Britain and in America at last, to note their activity in Macedonia. In the recent war Lydia would have been at home and a leader beyond a doubt.

She was not discounted in Philippi because she had a trade. Indeed, we may see the day when the idle woman is the one to be pitied and who has to apologize for her idleness. The chief business woman of the world is the one who manages her home successfully and within her husband's income, especially if he happens to be a preacher. She is the excellent woman of Proverbs 31:

> "Her clothing is fine linen and purple.
> Her husband is known in the gates."

It is not known whether Lydia was married or not. If so, she was probably a widow. But certainly her husband would have said of her:

> "Many daughters have done worthily,
> But thou excellest them all."

II. A ZEALOUS PROSELYTE OF THE GATE

She was "one that worshipped God" (Acts 16:14). This is the technical description of the "God-fearers" or proselytes of the gate, as the later rabbinic language has it. Cornelius is so described (Acts 10:2, 22). See also Acts 13:16, 26, 50, etc. They stood at the gate, but had not formally entered into Judaism by the rite of circumcision. They were no longer polytheists, but were devout worshippers of the one true God. They attended the synagogue worship and contributed liberally to its support. And yet they ranked not technically as Jews in all ceremonial matters, for they had not taken the final step. So Peter apologizes for entering the house of Cornelius (Acts 10:28).

It is from these "God-fearers" that Paul usually wins his first converts from the Gentiles. So it is in Philippi. His first convert in Europe is a woman and a proselyte of the gate.

Lydia may have become interested in Judaism in Thyatira, for there was a large Jewish colony there. The cult of Cybele flourished among the heathen in Thyatira and this voluptuous nature-worship led to much immorality. There, as elsewhere, the higher type of the heathen turned to Judaism for help in the world of darkness about them. Certainly Lydia was earnest in her interest in Judaism, since she and her group of women went all the way from Philippi to the river-side (the Gangas or Gangites) some miles away in order to worship God in the "place of prayer." This term is sometimes used for the synagogue and then again for any house or place when prayer is offered (3 Macc. 7:20). It is not possible to decide how it is employed here, though it may be noted that Luke has synagogue elsewhere as in Acts 17:1.

The location of the place of prayer so far from the city suggests that the Jews were a small group in Philippi. In Thessalonica they are a powerful body for it was a great commercial city. Philippi was a Roman colony and a sort of military outpost.

The river was convenient for the ceremonial ablutions of the Jews. But the point to note about Lydia is that she took the trouble to go to this out-of-town place of prayer to worship God with a small body of Jews. There were plenty of excuses that she could have found for not going whether she walked or rode a donkey. But she went. In these days of slackness about attendance at public worship the example of Lydia, the proselyte of the gate, is quite pertinent.

We are not surprised to find that Paul and his company went out there, even though it was not certain that there was a place of prayer in that locality. They "supposed" it to be there (Acts 16:13) and went on in the hope of finding it.

III. LISTENING TO THE TRAVELLING JEWISH PREACHER

We do not know what it was that caught Lydia's attention in Paul's message. It was a common thing in the synagogues for the Jewish stranger present to be given an opportunity to speak a word of exhortation. At Antioch, in Pisidia, "after the reading of the law and the prophets the rulers of the synagogue sent unto them (Paul and Barnabas), saying, brethren, if ye have any word of exhortation for the people, say on." There by the river-side at the place of prayer no such formality may have been observed.

The fact that only women are mentioned in attendance seems to imply that it was not a real synagogue out here by the river, but only a place for prayer and ceremonial ablutions. Philippi was a Latin town and few Jews were there. The rabbinical rule was that ten men were necessary to form a synagogue.

It looked like a poor opportunity for the great apostle to the Gentiles to make a beginning for the conquest of Europe. He had responded to the Macedonian cry and found no opening in Philippi at all. And there seemed to be small promise here. Some men would have returned to Philippi without preaching to this handful of Jewish women, some of them proselytes. Indeed, it is likely that it was more conversation than public address, for Luke says, "We sat down and spoke" (imperfect tense).

Perhaps each of the four (Paul, Silas, Timothy, Luke) engaged in conversation with a separate woman. Paul spoke to Lydia and by and by all may have listened. I heard D. L. Moody say that he knew of more souls saved by his conversation than by his preaching. One recalls Jesus and Nicodemus, and Jesus and the Samaritan woman at Jacob's well. It is more spectacular to deliver a public address and this has to be done. But it should never be above the will of the greatest preacher to talk to a single person about his salvation.

Lydia was at once interested in what Paul had to say. She kept on listening (imperfect tense). Paul was no doubt eager to win this woman to Christ. He did not feel that it was a small beginning. Missionaries to-day have to start their work in just this way. One wins one. And Lydia was eager to hear it all.

IV. LYDIA'S HEART OPENED

"Whose heart the Lord opened to give heed unto the things which were spoken by Paul." Paul soon saw that Lydia was deeply concerned in what he was saying. That is what stirs a preacher most, when he sees a soul responding to the word of God.

Luke says that "the Lord opened" Lydia's heart. That is God's part. But Lydia listened and gave heed. She did her part and gave the word of God a chance to do its work. It is certain that more people would have their hearts opened if they listened attentively to the message. It is a hard thing for most people to concentrate their minds upon a given proposition for a half hour or so. Few are willing to face squarely and frankly for one hour their personal relations to God.

It is a solemn thing to have to deal with a soul in such a plastic moment. A false note may repel the inquirer. The preacher must become a fisher of men. He must know how to draw the soul to Christ. We need not worry for fear that the Lord will not open the heart of the seeker after light. That is God's task and responsibility. Let us be sure that we do our full duty in making the way plain and in making Christ attractive to sinners.

It is not clear that Lydia was converted on this first visit of Paul to the place of prayer, though that was likely the case.

Paul had this ground of joy, he had won Lydia to Christ, but he did not know what a prize he had captured. She was a prophecy of the great army of noble women through the ages who would rally to the standard of Jesus in Europe and in America. Jesus was to set the women of the world free in due time. It was an historic occasion when Lydia gave her heart to Christ. Woman ·can never repay the debt that she owes to Christ.

V.   FOLLOWING HER LORD IN BAPTISM

Evidently Paul had spoken of baptism as the next step after conversion. Paul did not make baptism essential to salvation. He was not a sacramentarian as is plain from 1 Corinthians 1:17: "For Christ sent me not to baptise, but to preach the gospel." And yet Paul did not belittle baptism as of no significance. He found in it a picture of the heart of the gospel: "We were buried with him through baptism into death" (Rom. 6:4). So Lydia gladly submitted to this ordinance that in a mystic sense proclaimed death to sin and resurrection to the new life in Christ.

Probably Paul himself baptised her, though his rule was to leave the baptising to others (1 Cor. 1:16). There was apparently little delay on the part of Lydia. As yet no church seems to have been organized in Philippi, but that came soon.

VI. LEADING HER HOUSEHOLD WITH HER

Lydia's "household" was baptised also. That was true of the household of Cornelius (Acts 10:44, 47; 11:14), of the jailer (Acts 16:34), of Stephanas (1 Cor. 1:16), and of Crispus (Acts 18:8).

In the case of Lydia it is not clear whether she was married or not. The word for "household" may mean her servants or workwomen. Euodia and Syntyche may have been in the number. But it is certain that this noble woman exerted her influence to bring her household, whether children, domestics, or employees in her business, to the service of Jesus Christ. She set an example for all parents in the home life to lead children and servants to Christ. She is a rebuke to all heads of business establishments who are afraid to take a positive stand for Christ.

It is much easier to make a contribution for mission work somewhere else than it is to do the work that lies right before one's eyes. We are prone to be

cowardly before our own children and to be silent
about the life in Christ before those who work in our
homes, our store, our factories, or on our farms.
There is no better way to spread the power of Christ
than just this personal work with those near and dear
to us. If we take Christ into our hearts, we should
take him into our homes, and into our places of business. In the army religion has come to the front to
help the morale of the men who fight. None the less
do we need Christ in the quieter times of peace.

VII. THE GRACE OF HOSPITALITY

"If ye have judged me to be faithful to the Lord,
come into my house and abide there" (Acts 16:15).
Lydia was anxious to prove the sincerity of her conversion, as every new convert ought to feel. Gratitude to Christ prompts one to do something for His
cause. The time to take up the work is at once. Those
who put it off may drop back and then drop out. Lydia
saw this much that she could do at once. She had
wealth and a comfortable home. She probably had
servants to attend to the wants of her guests. So she
"besought us," Luke says, to come and to make her
home their home.

She wanted all four of them. Hospitality is one of
the finest Christian graces. It is commended and urged
in the New Testament. It is not possible for all to
do as much as Lydia in this respect. But hospitality
brings rich reward to those who can exercise it. Many
have entertained angels unawares. The sweetest
memories in many homes linger about the visits of
saints of God. The children carry with them through

life the impress of these visiting angels who show the courtesy of Christ. Many of the best homes in the world swing open to those who are the servants of Jesus.

It is evident that Paul was reluctant to accept the invitation of Lydia. There were four of the party and they would probably be in Philippi for some time. Paul was the most independent of men. He was the last man in the world to impose upon the generosity of others. He knew how to make his living so as to be free, as he did in Thessalonica, shortly afterward (2 Thess. 3:8). But Lydia was in earnest and she would take no refusal, especially on grounds like those just mentioned. "She constrained us," Luke says. Literally, "she forced us" to accept. She had her way in this matter, as she probably did in most things, for she had the gift of leadership.

Paul and his party were now in luxury. They richly deserved this generous treatment and they greatly enjoyed the charm of Lydia's home. Paul and Silas were soon to be thrown into prison in Philippi. Paul knew what rough handling was, for at Lystra he had been stoned and left for dead. Blessings on Lydia for giving some of the comforts of life to these servants of the Lord Jesus.

VIII. THE CHURCH IN HER HOUSE

"And they went out of the prison, and entered into the house of Lydia; and when they had seen the brethren, they comforted them, and departed" (Acts 16:40).

It is plain that the brethren and sisters, now a church

apparently, had met in Lydia's house during the time of the arrest of Paul and Silas. So in Jerusalem the home of Mary, mother of John Mark, had been the place of meeting as the saints prayed for Peter's release. It came to be a common thing for the believers to meet in the house of one who had a home capacious enough for that purpose. Lydia made her home the centre of Christian influence in Philippi.

When Christ comes into the home, some other things go out. That is one reason that some do not wish Him to come in. Family worship is a blessing to the home. Lydia became the dominant spirit in this new church in Philippi.

IX. THE CHURCH THAT CHEERED PAUL

Paul had much to try him in the churches that he founded as in Galatia and in Corinth. But the church in Philippi was the first that contributed to his missionary work and the most generous of all (Phil. 4:10-20). This was probably due to the enlightened liberality of Lydia. She had means, it is true. But not all Christians who have money have also the grace of liberality.

Lydia led the church out of the narrow selfishness that claimed so many. The story of Lydia has been repeated in the life of many churches since her time. Each of us can recall instances when the very life of the church turned upon the zeal of one woman. The men are hardened by love of money. The women are indifferent through love of worldly pleasures. One woman may have the insight and the courage to press on for higher things. In time the church will come to her ideals. Such a woman is the pastor's joy and hope.

Lydia was a promise of the great harvest that lay before Paul. Her noble spirit brightened his heart through dark days that were ahead. To be sure, Luke remained in Philippi several years. These two staunch friends of Paul moulded this church into a great missionary dynamo.

CHAPTER VIII

SILAS THE COMRADE

Our information about Silas or Silvanus (the longer form in the Epistles—1 Thess. 1:1; 2 Thess. 1:1; 2 Cor. 1:19; 1 Pet. 5:12), is not extensive and yet it is possible to get a pretty clear picture of him by piecing together the hints here and there in the Acts and the Epistles.

I. A HELLENIST AND A ROMAN CITIZEN

In these two respects he was like Paul. It seems clear from Acts 16:37, "being Romans," that Silas as well as Paul was a citizen of Rome. He also, like Paul, had a Latin name (Silvanus) and was evidently a Hellenist while Judas Barsabbas (Acts 15:22) was an Aramæan Jew, possibly brother of the Joseph Barsabbas of Acts 1:23. It has been argued that 2 Corinthians 1:19 and 8:23 make possible the identification of Silas with Titus. But, on the other hand, the picture of Titus in Galatians 2:3 is quite out of keeping with that in Acts 15 (Knowling). In Galatians 2:3 Titus is a Greek, while in Acts 15 Silas is a messenger from the Jerusalem church and one of their leaders. The suggestion that Silas is the author of the Epistle to the Hebrews is pure hypothesis with no convincing proof.

II. A JERUSALEM LEADER

He is described along with Judas Barsabas as "leading men among the brethren" (Acts 15:22). The word (ἡνούμενος) is a favorite one with Luke (Luke 22:26; Acts 7:10; 14:12), but does not specify the office or rank of Silas. He was one of the chief men and stood in the forefront when we first meet him in the Acts. He was apparently one of the elders of the church in Jerusalem. He is not mentioned by name in the discussions of the conference, though it is more than likely that he was present during the private conference called by Paul (Gal. 2:1-10), and he may have spoken in the public debate afterwards (Acts 15:7).

He was a man beyond a doubt who enjoyed the confidence of the Jerusalem church, of Paul and Barnabas, and of the church in Antioch. He was clearly not a Judaiser. As a Hellenist he belonged to the more liberal wing of the Jewish Christians like Paul and Barnabas, while Judas Barsabbas probably represented the more conservative element of Aramæan Christians under the lead of Peter, James, and John. Both sides were now united against the Judaisers and both sides were represented in the two ambassadors entrusted with the important letter to Antioch. It is a letter of commendation (Acts 15:27), probably written by James, like that carried by Saul from the Sanhedrin (Acts 9:2), and left matters of detail to be explained by Judas and Silas. The two commissioners are trusted ambassadors able to expound the will of the conference concerning the problem of Gentile freedom. The mission is a delicate and important one as this first Christian Epistle preserved to us shows, unless the Epistle of James antedates the conference. It is plain that Silas is a man of such parts and standing that his appointment gives satisfaction all around. Judas and Silas are qualified to interpret the Epistle (Acts 15:27).

III. A PROPHET IN ANTIOCH

The ambassadors fulfilled their function with eminent skill (Acts 15:30-33). They delivered the epistle to the new council (Rackham) assembled at Antioch. The letter was read aloud to the Greek multitude confirming their freedom from the Mosaic ceremonial law, though with proper emphasis on the moral code and with due recognition of the fact that Jewish Christians had perfect liberty to keep up the Mosaic ceremonial rules if they wished. The decision gave perfect liberty to the Gentile Christians, but left an occasion for further irritation between the Jewish and Gentile Christians in their social relations.

But the decree was wise in its caution and was still in force when Paul came to Jerusalem the last time, though Paul himself saw that only love, not knowledge and not law, could regulate the relation of Christians with each other (1 Cor. 8-10; Rom. 14 and 15). Finally, the author of Hebrews will call upon Jewish Christians to come clean out of the camp of Judaism and take their stand beside the Gentile Christians (Heb. 8-13). But now the Gentiles at Antioch are overjoyed at the confirmation of their own freedom; so they heard Judas and Silas with great delight as their "prophets," "exhorted the brethren with many words and strengthened them."

It was a new day for Christianity. The shadow of Pharisaism that had gathered over the Gentile churches was now removed. Silas evidently spoke with the prophetic spirit and encouraged and strengthened the spirits of the brethren. It was a crisis that called for courage and wisdom. If the Judaisers had wone, Christianity among the Gentiles would have dried up to a hardened type of Pharisaism or would have sloughed off from the Jewish trunk. But now the way for progress was open, but it called for prudence and restraint on the part of the Gentile Christians not to irritate the Jewish Christians needlessly.

It is to the credit of Silas and Judas that they entered heartily into the celebration of the Gentile victory at Antioch and remained long enough for them to know that the triumph was secure. There was prophecy and exhortation in Antioch as when Barnabas came from Jerusalem in the beginning (Acts 11:27, 28). Silas and Judas made "an earnest appeal for unity and mutual charity" (Rackham). The Bezan text in 15:34 says, "But it seemed good unto Silas to abide there and Judas returned alone." This is probably an effort to explain how Silas was later with Paul in Antioch (Acts 15:40). It is easy enough to understand that Silas came back to Antioch after the formal report to the Jerusalem church. There was time enough for this return in the "some days" of verse 36. Peace had come to the church at Antioch and Silas had been the bearer of glorious news. The gift of New Testament prophecy does not mean always technical prediction, though that was true of the prophet Agabus at Cæsarea (Acts 21:10, 11). In the case of Silas and Judas it is rather the gift of unctuous address under the guidance of the Holy Spirit, men endowed with the power of speaking the mind of the Spirit. The highest form of preaching may rise to the level of prophecy. Clearly Silas was a man of mark and a man of destiny.

IV.   THE CHOICE OF PAUL FOR HIS MISSION WORK

It was a shock to Paul and a blow to his hopes and plans when Barnabas pulled away from him and went to Cyprus with John Mark. Barnabas had been Paul's friend in the hour of need. He had befriended him in Jerusalem after his conversion when the rest eyed him with suspicion and distrust. He had brought him from Tarsus to Antioch when the work there called for another worker. He had stood by Paul when the leadership in the mission enterprise passed to his hands with no thought of jealousy. He had zealously championed Paul's fight for Gentile freedom in Antioch and in Jerusalem. In Jerusalem it was still "Barnabas and Paul" (Acts 15:25). But he would not stand for the abrupt brushing aside of John Mark because of his mistake at Perga. So the rift widened between these two servants of Christ. "Even Barnabas" had been led away from Paul at Antioch by Peter and probably John Mark (Gal. 2:13). That Paul had counted "hypocrisy," and now Barnabas was gone. The blow was serious to Paul's work and the heart-ache real.

Men Drop Out—God's Work Goes On

But no man is absolutely essential to the cause of Christ. The pastor who resigns in a hurry with the expectation of being asked to stay may do that once too often. His resignation may be accepted. His place will be filled. The work will go on. This is true in business and in statecraft. Paul had a man right at hand to take the place of Barnabas. Silas possessed many of the traits of the "son of consolation." He had influence in the Jerusalem church, though a Hellenist like Barnabas and a Roman citizen like Paul. He was in thorough sympathy with the onward movement of Christianity among the Gentiles as shown by his previous conduct. His leadership and prophetic gift gave him special adaptation for the missionary enterprise. It is clear that Silas accepted with alacrity the invitation of Paul to share his fortunes in the new tour. The sympathy of the church at Antioch was with Paul and Silas, "commended by the brethren to the grace of the Lord" (Acts 15:40).

So Paul went on through Syria and Cilicia strengthening the churches (Acts 15:14). Silas did not, of course, measure up to the stature of Barnabas in this new partnership. He was manifestly more Paul's helper and less Paul's equal, as they set out on the fresh campaign of world conquest for Christ. It was now specially Paul's campaign. He selected Silas as later he chose Timothy and Luke. But Silas will be no figurehead in their tour. He is already a man of experience and of prowess, but quite willing to take second place with Paul whom he evidently greatly admires. Harnack ("The Acts of the Apostles," p. 201) thinks that Silas was Luke's authority for the events at Jerusalem and Antioch in Acts 15. This may well be. Timothy came into the party (Acts 16:3) in

the place of John Mark and would take a lower place
than Silas. One of the notable things about Paul is
his skill in the choice of his co-workers. He loved
them and gloried in them. In return they showed
a firm spirit of loyalty and devotion. Paul gathered
round him a wonderful group of friends and workers
in the gospel.

V. PRISONER IN PHILIPPI

The narrative in Acts 16:19-40 shows that in the
eyes of the masters of the poor girl who had been
set free by Paul from the demoniac possessions, Silas
was equally guilty with Paul. The girl had described
"these men" (Paul, Silas, Timothy, Luke) as "slaves
of the most high God who proclaim to you a way of
salvation" (Acts 16:17). Paul spoke the word to
the spirit of evil in the girl (Acts 16:18). But the
girl's masters (κυριοι) laid hands on Silas as well
as Paul when they saw the hope of their gain from
the exploitation of the girl was gone. Perhaps they
saw that Silas was Paul's right-hand man and had expressed decided approval of Paul's conduct. Anyhow,
they try to implicate him as *particeps criminis* in the
loss of their business. This is primarily what concerned them and they wish to take their spite out on
both Paul and Silas. They may have hoped that with
Paul and Silas out of the way the girl would recover
her power of divination. They made no distinction
in the treatment of Paul and Silas and in the charges
made against them. They were both handled roughly
and dragged into the market-place before the magis-
trates (prætors). Their business had been hit as

was true later of Demetrius in Ephesus, but they do not tell the real cause of their complaint against Paul and Silas. They rather pose as patriots and make a grandstand play to the populace. It is patriotism for profit, but this they conceal by arousing race prejudice of Romans against Jews and accuse Paul and Silas with being law breakers (16:21). Judaism was a legal religion in the Roman Empire, but to persuade Roman citizens to adopt Jewish customs was not allowed (Rackham).

The charge was untrue in fact, and the obvious refutation was at hand since both Paul and Silas were Roman citizens themselves. It has often been asked why Paul and Silas did not lay claim to their Roman citizenship and put a stop to the alleged trial. Paul saved himself from scourging in Jerusalem by claiming his rights (Acts 22:25-29). Some say that Silas was not a Roman citizen and that Paul was silent to shield Silas. He was not willing to save himself and leave Silas in peril. But Paul expressly says in Acts 16:37 that both are Romans. The obvious explanation lies in the fact that the multitude gave them no opportunity to say anything in self-defense (Acts 16:22).

It was no trial at all, but a farce. The prætors ordered them to be scourged and put in prison without allowing Paul and Silas to say anything. This was done in response to the popular clamor caused by the adroit charge of the girl's masters. Paul seems to say precisely this in his dignified refusal to leave next morning after the earthquake and the conversion of the jailer. The prætors had evidently become uneasy

at their illegal conduct and sent sergeants to set the
men free. "They have beaten us," "men that are
Romans," says Paul (Acts 16:37). This was unlaw-
ful. One of the rights of Roman citizenship was
exemption from scourging. They have done it "publicly," an added indignity. They have "cast us into
prison" "uncondemned" or without a trial. The prætors were themselves in grave peril and Paul can afford
to demand a dignified dismissal at the hands of the
prætors themselves.

The Courage of Silas

The conduct of Silas during the imprisonment was
courageous. With their feet fast in the stocks "Paul
and Silas were praying and singing hymns unto God,
and the prisoners were listening to them" (Acts
16:25). It was a strange sound at midnight in that
prison and won an eager audience scattered in the
various cells. These were men who had praises to God
instead of curses for men. It was one way to preach
to these men by showing how the Christian can turn
trouble into joy and can make a prison the very gate
of heaven. One cannot think of Paul in the Philippian jail without seeing Silas with him, both happy
in the stocks, spite of bruised bodies and unknown ter-
rors on the morrow. They were happy when they
were with Jesus. The earthquake completed the conviction of the jailer who had been deeply moved by
the conduct of these strange prisoners who had manifestly mingled the gospel message with their songs
and prayers. He fell at the feet of both Paul and

Silas and asked what he must do to be saved (Acts 16: 29, 30).

It was a great triumph and Silas shared it with Paul. Henceforth Paul and Silas were linked together by this fellowship in suffering like soldiers in battle. This experience had knit their souls together. They knew that Jesus was with them in prison as really as at home. When they left Philippi next day, these two travellers on the road to Amphipolis and Thessalonica, they were brothers in Christ in a new way. Luke remained in Philippi, his probable home. Timothy apparently tarried for a while, but joined Paul and Silas in Berœa (Acts 17:14). Paul and Silas are refugees from the greed of men who will not submit calmly to the loss of revenue. It was the old fight of money against man. The welfare of the girl weighed nothing in the scale when the money was gone. That was heathenism—that is heathenism to-day, even if it appears in child labor or white slavery or brutal indifference to girls, women, and men in store and factory.

VI. AN EXILE FROM THESSALONICA

In Thessalonica Silas appears as the co-worker of Paul. Paul was the preacher, but Luke records that some of the hearers "consorted with Paul and Silas" (Acts 17:4). The jealousy of the Jewish rabbis was directed against both Paul and Silas. When they had gathered the crowd of "vile followers of the rabble" they went to Jason's house to fetch both Paul and Silas (Acts 17:5) apparently for the mob to lynch them. The charge laid at the door of Jason before the politarchs (technical name for the rulers of Thessalonica) is that he had entertained Paul and Silas, men who "act contrary to the decrees of Cæsar, saying that there is another king, one Jesus" (Acts 17:7). This religious rivalry leads the rabbis to pose as friends of Cæsar and opposed to political revolutionists like Paul and Silas. One is reminded of the like final threat to Pilate to tell Cæsar if he let Jesus free from the charge of claiming to be a king. They well knew that Jesus claimed to be a spiritual King as these rabbis probably understood the real meaning of Paul and Silas. But hatred grabs at every technicality.

Probably Paul in Thessalonica (see 2 Thess. 2) had laid some stress on the conflict between the Kingdom of God and the kingdom of this world. Certainly he was seeing the Roman Empire loom up as the very power of Antichrist. The conflict between Christ and Cæsar was very real in ideals and spirit. The upshot of it all was that, to release Jason from the bond which he had to give because of Paul and Silas, they both left Thessalonica for Berœa.

Silas and Paul Work Together

Silas was now in the full swing of Paul's missionary career and was only too glad to be with Paul during these days of severe trial. He was learning what it was to face the anger of Roman grafters in Philippi and the spite of jealous Jewish rabbis in Thessalonica as he had seen the biting bitterness of the Judaisers in Jerusalem. But it was all in the day's journey. The Judaisers might yelp at Paul's heels and the heathen and the Jew might bark at his onward march

but onward he would go. If not in one town, then
in the next. Paul and Silas left the gospel entrenched
in Thessalonia, as in Philippi, before they left. And
Paul kept up contact with the churches established.

VII. ON GUARD IN BERŒA

The story of Thessalonica was soon repeated in
Berœa. The success of the Jewish rabbis there soon
brought them to Berœa and Paul left, "sent forth"
by the brethren as far as Athens. But Silas and
Timothy (who has now come on from Philippi, probably with good things for Paul and Silas) "abode
there still" (Acts 17:14). This time the brethren evidently felt that it was enough for Paul to go. The
Jews would have a harder time in finding fault with
Silas and Timothy, now that the leader was gone.
And yet these two could firmly establish the work there.
Probably Paul had been in Berœa a shorter time than
in Thessalonica or Philippi. But Paul was not content in Athens without Silas and Timothy and sent
back word from Athens for these to come on to him
there with all speed (Acts 17:15). It is not clear
that they came, thought it seems likely that Timothy
came alone, leaving Silas in Berœa. Paul speaks of
sending Timothy from Athens to Thessalonica
(1 Thess. 3:1, 2). If so, Silas remained on guard
in Berœa for some while. He seems, however, to
have gone on to Thessalonica with Timothy whence
both went to see Paul in Corinth. It is plain that in
this period Silas had a ministry of more independent
responsibility as Paul's representative and agent. We
may be sure that he fulfilled it with fidelity.

VIII.   LAST WORK WITH PAUL IN CORINTH

"But when Silas and Timothy came down from Macedonia, Paul devoted himself to the word" (συνείχετο τῷ λόγῳ) with new freedom and great power, testifying to the Jews that Jesus was the Christ" (Acts 18:5).   In other words now Paul made fewer tents and did more constant preaching, with the result that matters came quickly to a crisis in Corinth and Paul had to move his preaching from the synagogue to the house of Titus Justus next door.   Here he labored with great blessing for a year and a half (Acts 18:11).   The part that Silas and Timothy played in this ministry is evident.   They had brought supplies from Macedonian churches so that Paul was not a burden to the critical Corinthians during these days (2 Cor. 11:7-10).   The church at Philippi was the first to help Paul in his missionary campaign (Phil. 4:15-16), doing it while Paul was in Thessalonica.   Probably Philippi, Thessalonica, and Berœa were now enlisted in the good work, the first missionary union in the history of Christianity.   Silas and Timothy were the bearers of this bounty and probably also the agents in uniting these churches in this cooperative effort.   Silas and Timothy helped Paul in the preaching in Corinth as he gladly acknowledged later (2 Cor. 1:19).   Both Silas and Timothy send salutations to the church in Thessalonica when Paul writes to them (1 Thess. 1:1; 2 Thess. 1:1).

When Paul left Corinth, he seems to have left Silas and Timothy there.   Timothy rejoined Paul later in Ephesus (Acts 19:22), but we have no further record of Silas in connection with Paul.   Some think that a break came between these two men, but that is a gratuitous suggestion. Paul's work had multiplied greatly. Men were needed at many points. It is quite possible that Silas remained in Ephesus till Apollos came or nearly till then. He does not appear in the troubles in Corinth after the arrival of Apollos.

IX. WITH PETER IN BABYLON (ROME)

Our last glimpse of Silas (Silvanus) is as the amanuensis of Peter and the bearer of the First Epistle from Rome to the provinces in Asia Minor (1 Pet. 5:12). It is likely that Silas, like Tertius in Romans 16:22, wrote out the Epistle for Peter. He may have been at liberty to touch up the phraseology and the result may represent something of his own style. Thus many explain the difference between the style of 1 Peter and 2 Peter (without the aid of an amanuensis). One need not think that Silas had deserted Paul because he is with Peter. The work of Paul and Peter ran parallel more and more. As John Mark was a comfort to both men, so Silas seems to have been. He was a comrade of the great and toiled with them worthily.

CHAPTER IX

TITUS THE COURAGEOUS

Not a great deal of attention is paid to Titus in modern books, and yet he played a not unimportant part in early Christian history. He is not mentioned in Acts by name, though probably included in the "certain others" of Acts 15:2. It is in 2 Corinthians, Galatians and the Pastoral Epistles that he is prominent.

A BROTHER OF LUKE

This is, at least, probable. It is curious, that in the Acts neither Luke nor Titus is mentioned by name. We can see why Luke should leave out his own name. If Titus was his brother, then we can understand the omission of his name also. In 2 Cor. 12:18 "the brother" naturally in the Greek means "his brother," as Professor A. Souter has shown. The same thing is probable in 2 Cor. 8:18. The book of Acts fails to reveal the part played by Luke and Titus in the life and work of Paul. The Epistles make us wonder why this omission exists when the other co-laborers of Paul receive frequent mention.

A REAL GREEK

Paul expressly states, Gal. 2:3, that Titus was a Greek. His name is Roman, like that of Paul, but that proves nothing as to his race. It has been held by some that Titus is merely another name for Timothy, Silas, or Titus Justus, but that idea has not gained credence. He was a pure Greek. If he was, as is probable, the brother of Luke, then it follows that Luke was also a Greek, not a Hellenistic Jew. He was one of the first fruits of the Greek world that made such a large contribution to early Christianity.

Jesus foresaw (see John 12) that the Greeks would come to him, but only as he drew them by the Cross. Paul sees that the Cross had broken down the middle wall of partition between Jew and Gentile. At any rate here is Titus, the Greek, who is a trusted interpreter of Christ to the Gentiles. And Luke, his brother, has given us the Greek scholar's view of Christ, Peter and Paul and others, of the origin of Christianity.

PAUL'S SON IN THE GOSPEL

"My true child after a common faith," Paul terms him, Titus 1:4. It is not known where his home was, but he went with Paul from Antioch to Jerusalem to the Conference, Gal. 2: 1-3: Acts 15:2, and was already an active participant in the life of the Greek Church at Antioch. He may have come into this church before the first mission tour, or he may have been a product of this campaign. At any rate, Paul picked him out as a recruit for Christ and he appears with Paul from time to time in his work, as we shall see. Paul kept a weather eye open for young ministers, and gathered a notable and noble company of them whom he trained to carry on the work with him and after him, 2 Tim. 2:1ff. A minister who has no sons in the gospel has failed in a large part of his work. It should be the policy of every preacher to pray and work for labourers for the harvest. A church that does not produce preachers is in reality a dying church without spiritual energy.

A FIREBRAND FOR THE JUDAISERS

This is the first time (Acts 15) that Titus appears in the Apostolic history. Paul mentions it a long time afterwards, unless, indeed, Galatians is the first of Paul's Epistles as Ramsay now holds. It can be readily perceived why Luke, who gives in Acts 15 the public aspects of the Conference in Jerusalem, should pass by the details of the private meeting of the leaders where Paul first carried his point and where the case of Titus was brought forward as involving the whole controversy. Paul and Barnabas had resented the insolent demand of the Judaisers, who had come from Jerusalem to Antioch, that the Gentile Christians should be circumcised after the custom of Moses, Acts 15:1ff. These meddlers had come without the approval of the Jerusalem Church, Acts 15:24, and Paul defied them. He determined to get the Jerusalem Church to disown them and to stand by the freedom of the Gentile Christians from the Mosaic rites and ceremonies. Paul took along Titus, who was probably appointed by the church. The very presence of Titus in the Conference at Jerusalem was intolerable to the Judaisers and to the compromising brethren who were in favor of smoothing things over. Paul's language in Gal. 2:3-5 is quite involved, probably a reflection of his vehement passion on the occasion and the desire

to be fair all around. It has been understood variously,
but the following is the most likely meaning. Some
of "the false brethren" (Judaisers) boldly demanded
that Titus be circumcised before he be allowed to
participate in the Conference, these "who came in
privily to spy out our liberty which we have in Christ
Jesus, that they might bring us into bondage," Gal.
2:4. The weaker brethren begged Paul "because of
the false brethren privily brought in" to yield this
point on condition that a resolution be passed guaran-
teeing liberty to the Gentile Christians. But Paul
would have no paper resolutions that were mere
scraps of paper to be violated when put to the test.
Titus was really a test case. The whole issue was
involved in him. Paul could not look his Gentile converts in the face with a set of solemn decrees in his
hand and the fact of surrender in the case of Titus
nullifying the words of freedom, so he took his stand
against the compromisers, "to whom we gave place
in the way of subjection, no, not for an hour; that
the truth of the Gospel might continue with you,"
Gal. 2:5. It was as serious a matter as that in Paul's
opinion. If Christ could not save Gentiles without
their becoming Jews, there was no Gospel of Grace at
all, but merely the imposition of the old legalism under
the form of Christianity. "But not even Titus who
was with me, being a Greek, was compelled to be
circumcised," Gal. 2:3. Courage won liberty for Titus
and so for all Gentiles. Evangelical Christianity, spiritual religion, was really at stake in this great controversy. Titus was the innocent *crux* of the matter
in Jerusalem. A cause is often summed up in a man.

Titus was a red rag to the Judaisers, but he was the flag of freedom for the Gentiles. Paul won Peter, John and James to his position. He already had Barnabas with him, so he carried the decision of the Conference and took Titus back with him as the badge of Gentile liberty.

PAUL'S AGENT IN THE GREAT COLLECTIONS

We catch glimpses of Titus later in Paul's life, particularly in 2 Corinthians. In chapter 8 Paul says that Titus "had made a beginning," 8:6, in the matter of the great collections for the poor saints in Jerusalem, and that it was a year ago, the very first effort in the campaign, and by you "who were the first to make a beginning a year ago, not only to do, but also to will," 8:10. Paul had boasted "that Achaia hath been prepared a year past and your zeal hath stirred up very many of them," 9:2.

Titus then was the first of Paul's agents to take hold of this great money-raising campaign that did so much to teach the early churches co-operation and practical fellowship. He was eminetly successful and won such a hearty response in Corinth that Paul used it to stir the churches of Macedonia to like activity. The churches in Achaia were a bit slow in paying their pledges and Titus had to be sent later to urge prompt payment. But Paul was proud of his agents in the collection and demanded for them full support from the churches, 2 Cor. 8:24. Some ministers have a dislike for the financial side of church work, but Paul shows no sympathy with such an attitude. In chapters 8 and 9 of 2 Corinthians he handles

the subject without gloves. Paul is full of gratitude
for the courage and skill of Titus in this campaign,
8:16. It is possible that on this first trip Titus did
not have to stay long.

PAUL'S CHAMPION IN CORINTH

Matters soon began to go wrong in Corinth because
of the Judaising agitators and the factions created in
the church, cf. 1 Cor. 1:10ff. These disturbances
probably go far towards explaining the non-payment
of the pledges made to Titus. Paul sent Timothy over,
but he seems to have failed to do much in the matter,
1 Cor. 4:17; 16:10. He may have made a short visit
himself, but he certainly wrote a letter to them before
our 1 Corinthians, 1 Cor. 5:9. He then wrote the
extended reply to all their inquiries and sent our 1 Corinthians. But Titus had to be sent also, for Timothy
brought back bad news. Titus may have carried the
sharp epistle mentioned in 2 Cor. 2:4 and 7:8-12, which
caused the Corinthians so much sorrow and gave Paul
real anguish of soul, being written in tears. But-
tressed by this powerful letter Titus stood the factions
down and won a clean victory for Paul. There was a
stubborn minority led by the Judaisers left. But the
four factions dwindled to two. It was now a clear-
cut issue with the Pauline party in full control. This
news Titus brought to Macedonia to Paul, who had
hurried over from Troas, tortured by anxiety and unable to wait there as by arrangement, 2 Cor. 2:12ff.
Titus comforted Paul greatly, 7:5-7. "Therefore we
have been comforted; and in our comfort we joyed
the more exceedingly for the joy of Titus because his

spirit hath been refreshed by you all," 7:13. Paul's heart ran over with joy at the victory of Titus in Corinth. It was good for them, too, to meet in the hour of triumph. It was natural for Titus to feel proud of the outcome in Corinth. Paul was glad that he had not lost his faith in the brethren there in spite of their factions. "For if in anything I have gloried to him on your behalf, I was not put to shame; but as we spake all things to you in truth, so our glorying also which I made before Titus was found to be truth," 7:14. Paul wishes to assure the Corinthians of Titus' affection for them. "And his affection is more abundantly toward you, while he remembereth the obedience of you all, how with fear and trembling ye received him," 7:15. Evidently there had been moments of uncertainty and of uneasiness, but it had now turned out all right through the tact of Titus and their own rightmindedness. "I rejoice that in everything I am of good courage concerning you," 7:16. So then Titus had met every expectation of Paul in this crisis of affairs at Corinth. He had routed ·the Judaisers as Paul had done in Jerusalem, all but the stubborn minority. And Titus was the man to tackle them.

THE THIRD VISIT TO CORINTH

One good turn deserves another. Nothing succeeds like success. So Paul writes our 2 Corinthians, for the integrity of this epistle is still on the whole probable. The first part explains Paul's elation at the victory of Titus and expresses Paul's gratitude over the attitude of the majority. Chapters 8 and 9 take up the matter of paying the pledges of a year ago, the way for which is now clear. Titus is to go back to Corinth for this purpose with two other brethren, probably Luke and Erastus, Acts 19:22. Timothy did not go, but sent his greetings along with those of Paul, 2 Cor. 1:1. Paul pleads for a kind reception for Titus, his personal representative, and for the other two messengers ("apostles") of the churches, 8:18-24. He plans to come later himself, and does not wish any Macedonians to find them still behind with the money, 9:3ff. Titus probably took with him our 2 Corinthians, which also has a plain warning to the Judaising minority, 10-13, and a threat of sterner measures when Paul does come if they are needed. Paul then goes round about to Illyricum, Rom. 15:19, and waits for Titus to do this finishing job in Corinth. It was superbly done so far as we can judge, for Paul later spent three months there, Acts 20:3, without serious opposition from Judaisers, though the Jews made a plot against him as he was leaving.

THE EVANGELIST IN CRETE

We hear no more of Titus for some ten years, not till after Paul's visit to Jerusalem, the imprisonment in Cæsarea and in Rome, and the release. Paul writes a short letter to Titus whom he had left in Crete, Titus 1:5. So then Titus had another ministry with Paul here. Paul apparently had to leave the island before the work of organisation was complete. He left the finishing of this work in the hands of Titus. He was to set in order things there and to appoint elders in every city, just like a modern missionary in a heathen land. Paul seems familiar with conditions in Crete and gives Titus careful directions how to meet the peculiar problems of his field there. A form of Pharisaic gnosticism had gotten a foothold, and it fell in with the follies and weaknesses of the Cretan temperament as their own poet had said, 1 :10-16. "Let no man despise thee," 2 :15. Titus was to show the same courage that he had manifested in Corinth. We may be sure that Titus did not disappoint Paul in dealing with the sins of the various social groups in the churches of Crete, 2 :1-14, and in the selection of men who had the proper qualifications for the ministry, 1 :7-9. Factious men must be dealt with sharply, 3 :10ff, as Titus had learned how to do in Corinth. Titus came to be regarded as the patron saint in Crete, and his tomb was long believed to be at Gortyna, though that is by no means certain. He did not remain in Crete as we know.

FURTHER PLANS FOR TITUS

Paul apparently sent the letter to Titus by Zenas the lawyer, and Apollos, Titus 3 :13, who were to carry on the work in Crete, while Titus was to join Paul in Nicopolis before winter, 3 :12. We do not know, of course, whether Titus was able to join Paul then, but there is no particular reason to think otherwise. We do know that he was with Paul shortly before he wrote his last letter to Timothy, 2 Tim. 4 :10, for Paul expressly states that Titus had left for Dalmatia. There is no indication that Titus had deserted Paul in his hour of peril in Rome as Demas had done. Rather it appears that he was Paul's messenger from

Rome to the churches in Dalmatia, the lower part of
Illyricum, probably to the field that Paul had himself
once visited, Rom. 15:19. To the last Paul was full
of plans for pushing on the work of the kingdom. At
the very time he is pleading with Timothy to pick
up Mark and come to him in his loneliness, he is dis-
patching Crescens to Galatia and Titus to Dalmatia.
The work must go on and merely personal considerations must give way to the interests of the kingdom.
This is the spirit of the general. Titus responded to
the brave spirit of Paul and did his part to the end.
We know nothing more of Titus. We may be sure
that he did not lose heart when the final blow fell
upon Paul. He was a man of force, who knew how
to drive things through, a lieutenant to be trusted at
a critical moment, a man to be counted on in an emergency. It is good to know that there are always men
who will leap to the fore when the captain falls and
rally the men to the colours. Titus first comes on the
scene as a sort of stormy petrel in Paul's life. He
was with him to the finish and felt only that he did a
day's work as he met it. Paul thanked God for Titus,
"My true child after a common faith."

CHAPTER X

TIMOTHY THE FAITHFUL

Paul loved Timothy with the utmost devotion. He was more tender and sympathetic than Titus, though not so forceful. He was probably not so gifted or so cultured as Luke, but he was equally loyal and loving.

HIS GREEK FATHER

This is all that is told about his father, Acts 16:1. He was hardly a proselyte, for Timothy had not been circumcised before he became a Christian. He may have been one of the devout Greeks like Cornelius who attended the synagogue. It is hardly likely that he was an aggressive heathen who made things uncomfortable at home. The rather, it seems clear, that the Greek father left the training of Timothy to the mother and grandmother. But Timothy could not fail to receive some impress from Greek culture of the time through his father. The home was in Lystra in Lycaonia, and was on one of the great Roman thoroughfares between the east and the west.

A HOME OF PIETY

His mother was "a Jewess that believed," Acts 16:1, when Paul and Barnabas first came to Lystra. Timothy and she may have been in that circle of disciples who stood round Paul's body in fear that he was dead,

Acts 14:19f, when the mob had dragged him out of the city and left him. His mother's name was Eunice and his grandmother was Lois, who saw to it that Timothy was reared in the faith of his Jewish fathers, 2 Tim. 1:5. No doubt these good women took extra pains beyond the legal commands because of the Greek influence on his life. They taught him the Holy Scriptures from a babe, 2 Tim. 3:15. Paul could remind Timothy of his great privilege in this regard and urge fidelity to such teaching, 2 Tim. 1:5; 3:14. It is impossible to overestimate the value of teaching children the Bible.*

One reason why people know so little about the Scriptures is just that they do not learn the Bible in childhood.

A DISCOVERY OF PAUL'S

Paul was on the constant lookout for young preachers. He saw the tremendous demand for them if Christianity was to grow and extend over the world. Jesus had sorrowed as he saw the harvest ripe and the labourers so few, Matt. 9:37f. Timothy was converted during the first mission and was one of Paul's converts because he called him "my true child in faith," 1 Tim. 1:2; "my child Timothy," 1:18; "my beloved child," 2 Tim. 1:2; "my beloved and faithful child in the Lord," 1 Cor. 4:17. When Paul came to Lystra on the second mission tour, "him would Paul have to go forth with him," Acts 16:3. This was after the break between Paul and Barnabas over John Mark when Paul and Silas started out together, 15:36-40. At

* Mrs. Ella B. Robertson has made a volume of selections for children called "The Heart of the Bible" (Nelson's Sons).

Lystra, Timothy was picked up and was with Paul for most of his ministry while Mark had varying fortunes and final success with Barnabas and Peter and again with Paul. Few things in Paul's life gave him more comfort than the finding of Timothy. He had been educated as a Jew, and yet was not a Jew. Paul knew how to fight for principle, as in the case of the Greek Titus, but he knew also how to smooth out difficulties when no principle was involved. Timothy was neither Jew nor Greek, and so would be constantly objectionable to the Jewish Christians. So Paul "took and circumcised him because of the Jews that were in those parts; for they all knew that his father was a Greek," 16:3. Paul felt no inconsistency at all in this conduct and that about Titus, for "as they went on their way through the cities, they delivered them the decrees to keep that had been ordained of the apostles and elders that were at Jerusalem," 16:4. Probably before going on with the tour, the ordination servive took place for inducting Timothy into the ministry. There is not a great deal said about ordination in the New Testament, but Timothy's case seems clear. Paul prided himself to a degree on his insight into Timothy's character at the first. He saw the promise that was in this gifted youth. He reminds Timothy that he "stir up (literally keep ablaze) the gift of God that is in thee through the laying on of my hands," 1 Tim. 1:6. Alas, how often is it true that the young minister lets the fire burn low, the flame of the Lord fresh from the altar. Paul was greatly exercised that Timothy keep up his habits of study and devotion. It is seldom that more wisdom for a young minister is found in fewer words than these of Paul to Timothy, "Till I come, give heed to reading, to exhortation, to teaching. Neglect not the gift that is in thee which was given thee by prophecy, with the laying on of the hands of the presbytery. Be diligent in these things; give thyself wholly to them; that thy progress may be manifest unto all. Take heed to thyself, and to thy teaching. Continue in these things; for in doing this thou shalt save both thyself and them that hear thee," 1 Tim. 4:13-16. From the ordination service on through the years Paul had Timothy on his heart and tried to steer his course aright. But there was no patronising of Timothy by Paul. He spoke of him to others in the noblest way as, "our brother and God's minister in the Gospel of Christ," 1 Thess. 3:2; "for he worketh the work of the Lord as I also do," 1 Cor. 16:10; "Timothy our brother," 2 Cor. 1:1; Col. 1:1; Philemon 1, "Paul and Timothy, slaves of Jesus Christ," Phil. 1:1; "Timothy my fellow-worker," Rom. 16:21. Paul's protégé became his co-worker on the level of high service for Christ.

NOT WITHOUT HONOUR AT HOME

Jesus found that a prophet had no honour at home according to the proverb. Nazareth twice cast him out. Many a young preacher has had to make a start in spite of the indifference, scepticism, or even ridicule of neighbours, or, alas, of the family circle. Jesus himself tasted that bitter cup. But Timothy "was well reported of by the brethren that were at Lystra and Iconium" when Paul came. He had apparently already made a beginning in active service for Christ.

These timorous first efforts were kindly received. In writing to Timothy later on the qualifications of the minister Paul will say, "Moreover he must have good testimony from them that are without," 1 Tim. 3 :7. It is hard to judge human nature at best and one's reputation is some guide to his worth, though it alone is not decisive. Character and reputation, alas, do not always correspond. But it speaks volumes for Timothy that his neighbours and friends were so cordial in their commendation to Paul. Paul will one day write to Timothy, "This charge I commit unto thee, my child Timothy, according to the prophecies which led the way to thee, that by them thou mayest war the good warfare," 1 Tim 1 :18. Hymenæus and Alexander made shipwreck, as so many since have done, of all the blessed hopes and promises of youth.

HIS FIRST CAMPAIGN WITH PAUL

Timothy held a subordinate place in the company of four (Paul, Silas, Timothy, Luke). After Paul and Silas were released from prison in Philippi, Timothy remained awhile with Luke. He soon rejoined Paul in Thessalonica as the bearer of gifts from Philippi to the Apostle, Phil. 4 :16, the first help of the kind that came to Paul in his great enterprise, Phil. 4 :15. Timothy and Silas remained in Berœa when Paul fled to Athens, Acts 17 :14 f., but Paul sent word for them to come on to Athens. Timothy apparently did come, but was sent back to Thessalonica by Paul, 1 Thess. 3 :1f., because of disturbances there concerning Paul's teaching about the second coming of Christ. Timothy and Silas later came to Corinth with more gifts from Philippi and also Thessalonica and Berœa, 2 Cor. 11:8f.; 1 Thess. 3:6; Acts 18.5. The gifts were gracious and in sharp contrast to the stinginess and slanders of the Corinthians, and Paul was comforted by the glad tidings from Thessalonica and "devoted himself to the word," Acts 18:5, with great power. There it will be seen that Timothy was useful to Paul during the great days in Macedonia and Achaia.

TIMOTHY IN CORINTH

Timothy was with Paul during most of the third mission tour. While at Ephesus the troubles at Corinth reached a crisis. Paul had various communications with the Church at Corinth in an effort to settle the troubles then. Finally he sent Timothy, "For this cause have I sent unto you Timothy, who is my beloved and faithful child in the Lord, who shall put you in remembrance of my ways which are in Christ, even as I teach everywhere in every church," 1 Cor. 4:17. Meanwhile he wrote 1 Corinthians and endorsed Timothy as his personal representative with full power to speak authoritatively for Paul as the passage just quoted shows. Paul put his whole case into the hands of Timothy. But he was evidently afraid that Timothy would not be able to harmonise the turbulent factions. As things stand in Corinth Paul has influence only with the Pauline party. "Now if Timothy come, see that he be with you without fear; for he worketh the work of the Lord, as I also do; let no man therefore despise him. But set him forward on his journey in peace, that he may come unto me; for I expect him with the brethren," 1 Cor. 16:10f. It seems plain that

Paul's fears were well grounded. Timothy came back
all right to Ephesus, but the storm raged on in Corinth,
and Paul sent Titus to see what he could do. Titus
took hold with energy and had great news for Paul
when he met him in Macedonia, 2 Cor. 12ff.; 7:6ff.
Apparently the Judaisers brushed Timothy rudely
aside as a stripling. Later Paul will say to Timothy,
"Let no man despise thy youth," 1 Tim. 4:12, perhaps with a recollection of the experience in Corinth.

But Timothy was true blue and gave Paul the best
that was in him. He was faithful when others flickered.
Paul, while a prisoner in Rome, was anxious to send
Timothy to Philippi, for "ye know the proof of him,
that, as a child serveth a father, so he served with me
in furtherance of the gospel," Phil. 2:22. Timothy
probably lacked genius, but he had goodness. He
was "a good minister of Jesus Christ," 1 Tim. 4:6.
Timothy had his "deposit" from God, 1 Tim. 6:20; 2
Tim. 1:14. Paul was anxious that the investment
that God had made in Timothy should not be in vain,
so he urged him to keep God's deposit. But, when
the test comes, Paul says, "I have no man likeminded
who will care truly for your state. For they all seek
their own, not the things of Jesus Christ," Phil. 2:20f.
He could count on Timothy to the limit. He could
trust him anywhere and all the time. That is loyalty,
and loyalty is "probably the fundamental trait in character" (Royce). Timothy would stand true when
others had deserted. Luke, likewise loyal, was probably not in Rome at this time.

IN CHARGE AT EPHESUS

After Paul's release from the first Roman imprisonment, he went east, then west, and then east again. He left Timothy in charge at Ephesus on his second visit east, 1 Tim. 1:3. It was a heavy responsibility for Timothy to have charge of the great church in Ephesus. But he no doubt measured up to it. Paul went on to Macedonia and wrote to Timothy a letter full of instructions for his guidance in the work there. Apparently Paul had not had time to go over all the details with Timothy. For this reason we have 1 Timothy, which is a rich storehouse for every minister to-day. There is a wonderful combination of personal directions about health, study, and piety along with ecclesiastical problems and doctrinal issues. "Paul the aged" writes with repose and grace, and yet with tenderness and force, sympathy and courage. He is still grateful to Christ for putting Paul, himself, into the ministry, 1 Tim. 1:12f. He is anxious that Timothy shall come up to the highest standard as a good minister of Christ, as a man of God, brave and strong to the end, 1 Tim. 1:18-20; 3:14ff.; 4:6-16; 5:21; 6:11, 20f. Paul is anxious concerning Timothy's health. He apparently was a nervous dyspeptic and Paul recommends "a little wine for thy stomach's sake and thine often infirmities," 5:23. There is nothing here against the strictest temperance or even prohibition, for modern medical skill has found other things better for the digestion than the "little wine." But preachers in poor health may find comfort in the case of Timothy. He held on and did a noble work in spite of his physical infirmities.

One must not pride himself on his poor health as a proof of piety. The poor, sickly preacher may be no whit more pious than his robust, athletic brother. Titus was no less pious than Timothy and more effective, sooth to say. But the preacher with a weak stomach need not despair of usefulness.

LONGED FOR BY PAUL

Paul is in prison for the last time. He knows what the outcome will be. He is no longer in his own hired house, but in the Mamertine Prison. Friends no longer came to see Paul, for it was now not safe to do so. Onesiphorus oft refreshed Paul by his courage till he was apparently slain for his daring, 2 Tim. 1:16-18. Timothy is still in Ephesus, but Paul longs for him to come to him before winter, 2 Tim. 4:21. He wishes him to pick up John Mark and bring him along also, 4:11, for the once useless minister has now made good and is useful to Paul (Robertson, "Making Good in the Ministry"). Paul needs his cloak which he left at Troas with Carpus, 4:13. But most of all he misses his books, especially the parchments, his own books which he had used through the years, his old books, in particular, copies of portions of the Old Testament, and perhaps even Mark's Gospel and Luke's writings. But, while Paul's heart aches for the presence and sympathy of Timothy, he is not unmindful of Timothy's own needs in Ephesus. This last message of Paul is full of courage: "For God gave us not a spirit of fearfulness (cowardice), but of power and love and discipline," 2 Tim. 1:7. He urges Timothy not to be ashamed of

Christ or of Paul, but to suffer hardships along with
Paul as a good soldier of Christ, 2 Tim. 1:8; 2:3-13.
Remember Christ and remember Paul. He urges that
Timothy keep himself in trim for his great task by
full knowledge of the Scriptures, 2:14f., and by clean
living, 2:20-26, and so escape the snare of the devil.
Paul is afraid of the devil's traps for preachers. Im-
postors must needs come, but the man of God must
know the Scriptures and be furnished completely unto
every good work, 3:15-17. The preacher does not
always feel fit for his task, but in season and out of
season Timothy must preach the word and not tickle
the itching ears of the fickle crowd with new fancies
and foibles. Paul sees the end of his course and he
is ready to go and receive his crown, 4:6-8. But he
wants to see Timothy before the Lord Jesus takes him
to his heavenly kingdom.

IN PRISON FOR PAUL

It is probable that Timothy came quickly to Paul
and paid the penalty for his courage by getting thrown
into prison himself. At any rate the writer of the
Epistle to the Hebrews says: "Know ye that our
Brother Timothy hath been set at liberty, with whom,
if he come shortly, I will see you," Heb. 13:23. We
may suppose therefore that Paul had the comfort of
Timothy's presence with him when the end came.
Probably Luke, Timothy, and Mark were those who
had the wonderful privilege of accompanying Paul to
the place of execution outside of Rome. We do not
know the further work of Timothy. We may be sure
that he held true to the last. He was a man of emotion

and sympathy, for Paul spoke of his tears, 2 Tim. 1:4. In all things he was "an ensample to them that believe, in word, in manner of life, in love, in faith, in purity," Tim. 4:12. He deserved Paul's love and confidence. Paul looked to him with hope for the future. "And the things which thou hast heard from me among many witnesses, the same commit thou to faithful men, who shall be able to teach others also," 2 Tim. 2:2. Thus the good work goes on. Teach the teachers. Pass on the teaching. "Hold the pattern of sound words which thou hast heard from me in faith and love which is in Christ Jesus," 2 Tim. 1:13.

CHAPTER XI

THOMAS THE PREACHER WITH HONEST DOUBTS

We seem to be entering an age of credulity, if one thinks of the great scientist, Sir Oliver Lodge, as a champion of actual communication with the dead. Certainly we have passed through an age of criticism of all that was outside of the laws of the physical universe as known by modern scientists. The transition has not come suddenly. Evolution itself has played some part in the change. It is a long step from the cold materialism of Darwin to the militant spiritualism of Lodge. And yet Lodge is an evolutionist. The veil between matter and mind has worn thin in places, to say the least, by reason of new discoveries like radium, wireless telegraphy, transmutation of metals, the breaking up of the atom into electrons, Einstein's theory of the gravitation of the light rays. In biblical criticism we have seen the same relentless search for facts. Tradition has stepped aside while the scholar, like the scientist in the laboratory, put in the crucible of criticism the cherished convictions of Christendom. The books of the Old Testament and of the New Testament have been subjected to the most minute dissection and the most careful literary analysis. The dry bones of redactors have rattled in the place of the mighty spirits of the Scriptures. We are coming again to the age of reconstructions and the dry bones are beginning to take on the form of life. But, meanwhile, many a minister has suffered the lapse of faith between the novelties of criticism of the Bible and the stern realities of inexorable scientific law. The modern minister has wished to face all the facts of life with open mind and heart. He has wished to be loyal to his Lord and to be a leader of his fellow men. He has not been desirous of being an obscurantist or a reactionary. It has often been the most sensitive spirits that have suffered most. The passion for truth and honesty of purpose has clashed with the traditions of environment. Some few who have been unable to place the Christ of the Gospels and of Paul's Epistles in the world of science and of criticism have either given up the ministry or have become Unitarian ministers. Others have lived down their doubts by deeper study and by patient waiting for further light that has come from Christ as it came to Thomas.

Thomas is the typical preacher who has struggles with honest doubts. This is partly due to temperament, but one cannot easily change his temperament whether phlegmatic or bilious or nervous. Thomas had his pessimistic moods. He saw at once and sharply the difficulties in the way. He was unwilling to shut his eyes to the actual facts that confronted him. His first reaction was despondency. He came through in the end, but he had to fight his way through the fog and smoke to the light. Thomas was an outspoken man, besides, who in a rather blunt manner spoke out his mind. Such a man often reflects the feelings of

others who receive credit for more faith than they
really possess and he also betrays more doubt than
he really feels. The Fourth Gospel alone gives us
an insight into the mind of Thomas as he faced the
problem of Christ during Passion Week and afterward.
Thomas reveals the courage of despair in John 11:6,
when he proposes to his fellow-disciples, "Let us also
go, that we may die with him." Jesus had just said
that Lazarus was dead. He had suggested going
to Bethany over the protest of the disciples that Jesus
might be killed; for the enemies of Jesus had tried
to stone him when he was last in Jerusalem, at the
feast of dedication (John 10:31). To Thomas it
seemed sheer madness for Jesus to go back into the
lions' den. Lazarus was dead. The rulers will kill
Jesus if he goes. And yet Thomas is the man who
takes his courage in his hands and proposes, not desertion of Jesus, but loyalty to him even unto death.
But he expects death for all of them. Thomas is
willing to go over the top, but he anticipates death
for all of the band in the going. It may be said that
this is not the highest form of courage, but it is courage. It is not reckless daring, but the looking of all
probabilities in the face. Thomas does not expect
success. He expects that the proposed visit to Bethany
will culminate in the death of Jesus and all the twelve.
He pleads that they may all be willing to make this
supreme sacrifice for the sake of the Master. It will
be an end, to be sure, to all their cherished hopes about
the Messianic Kingdom. They will all have to give
up their dreams of place and power in that kingdom.
They will not see Rome driven out of Palestine and

Jesus King in Jerusalem. It is a rude awakening for Thomas. Doubtless there is an implied rebuke to Jesus in the resignation of Thomas to the rashness of Christ. But, at any rate, he regards the situation as hopeless in view of the determination of the Master.

Ministers to-day have sometimes found themselves in a predicament where they had lost heart and hope in their work. They whipped themselves to their task with the courage of despair. The onward march of events has been against their predilections and prejudices, and even their principles. Some of the noblest of men have had to decide whether to "carry on" to the end with those who would not heed their advice or to quit and be termed slackers or even deserters. Thomas was not a quitter at any rate. He proposed to see the thing through even if his gloomiest forebodings came true. It is true that some ministers have found themselves out of sympathy with their age and unable to make much of an impression upon those who had swept on to other modes of thought. Who, then, is the prophet? Prophets have often had to denounce their age. Jesus did precisely this thing. And yet Jesus was the iconoclast and did not shrink from going on, not till he came to his own Gethsemane. I wish to make a plea for the preacher who in a troubled time has yet held on to his task in spite of discouragement and even despair. He has held on from the sense of duty that drives the soldier to the field of battle. It is easier to throw stones at such a man than to stand in his tracks. This is not to advocate the idea that a man who no longer believes in the deity of Christ should continue to preach it, or to occupy an evangelical pulpit or theological chair. The courage of despair is consistent with honest doubt, but not with loss of faith in Christ. Courage calls for honesty. When one has made his choice firmly and clearly he should take his stand. He should not stay within the lines and fire at his Captain.

The next time that Thomas comes before us is in John 14:1-7. Here Thomas exhibits the agnostic attitude toward death and the future life: "Lord, we know not whither thou goest; how know we the way?" (John 14:5). This bold avowal of ignorance of the future life after death follows the most intimate, tender, and precious promise of Jesus that he would come again and take them to the Father's house and to himself in the Father's home. He had urged faith in himself as in the Father and had pointedly stated that the disciples had grounds for confident fidelity since they knew the place and the way to the new abode: "And whither I go, ye know the way" (John 14:4). It is precisely at this point that Thomas interposes with his almost brutal statement of crass ignorance about both the location of the Father's house and the way thereto.

Once more Thomas is modern in his outlook and seems to voice the doubts of the present-day scientist who scans the heavens in vain for a planet that can be a fit abode for the spirits of the blest. The myriad blazing suns of the skies would seem more like the infernal regions than the home of Christ with the Father. Thomas was frankly puzzled as he tried to form an intellectual concept of the hope of heaven held out by Jesus in the words that have comforted the dying through all the ages since that night when Jesus spoke them. Thomas was face to face with the death of Jesus and the blasting of all his hopes. He longed for something more than figures of speech. He found the age-long question, Does death end all? Jesus had answered with the definite promise that he would come and take the disciples to the heavenly home. But the appeal to their knowledge gave Thomas his chance to confess his real ignorance. Many a preacher has brought comfort to the dying with the words of Jesus who has longed for more assurance in his own heart. The answer of Jesus to Thomas is still the best answer to the modern agnostic. It is easy to find fault with those who are driven by the terror of death to find light in the darkened chambers of so-called mediums. I am slow to believe that the Christian has need to resort to the devious ways of paid professional mediums with all the proven fraud to their credit and inanities in their so-called messages. Jesus spoke to Thomas the word that preacher and layman need today: "I am the way, and the truth, and the life: no one cometh unto the Father but by me" (John 14:6). Turn from mediums to Jesus. He is the expression of the Father in human form. He is the incarnation of the truth about the future life. He is, in fact, the life itself, the source of all energy and power. He is the Lord of life and death. He is the way to the Father. Jesus is the way; He, and not a system of science or of theology; He, and not an ecclesiastical organization; He, and not priest or medium.

Materialism has had a powerful grip upon some

minds during the nineteenth century. There are those to-day who can find no proof in the universe of mind apart from matter, who regard mind or spirit as a mere brain-function, who consider mind the product of matter, who hold that matter is eternal and mind merely the phosphorescent fire that flashes in the darkness and at death goes out forever. It is not easy to answer all the difficulties raised by materialism. There are things to be said that lead one out and on to the spiritual interpretation of the universe. Jesus himself has to be accounted for. The spirit of man refuses to believe that man is a mere lump of clay. It is not easy to believe in the eternity of matter that was never created and that was always endowed with the energy of life. The upward trend of life argues for the existence of God. Evolution itself calls for a higher order in the universe than man's life on earth. The agnostic can never be wholly answered. Thomas did not reply to Jesus, but he had the only real answer. It is Jesus. The minister who loses his way in life has lost his touch with Christ. Jesus alone is the door to the temple of knowledge. One must try Jesus. Christ lamented that Thomas had failed to see the Father in himself. There are those who do see God in Christ. He is the only path by which men can come to God.

The next time that we see Thomas in John's Gospel (20:25) the other disciples are saying to him, "We have seen the Lord." It is a marvellous statement. With the rest Thomas had passed through the gloom of that terrible Sabbath day when they had all suffered the eclipse of faith that followed the death of Christ. The Cross had destroyed faith and hope. All that they had finally dreamed and trusted was now buried in the tomb of Jesus. Thomas with the other disciples had heard the stories of Mary Magdalene and the other women, but they treated them as idle tales of excitable women about seeing angels, and in the case of Mary Magdalene as a probable recurrence of her demoniacal possession. So Thomas was somewhat taken aback by the sudden avowal of faith in the resurrection of Jesus by the very men who had so recently emphasised their disbelief in the reports of the women. Evidently the disciples proceeded to give various details about the appearance of Jesus on that first Sunday night when Thomas was absent (John 20:24). The new converts were full of faith, but they lacked the power to convince a sceptic like Thomas, who still had all the sceptic's distrust of supernatural phenomena. Thomas was not to be taken in by ghost stories. Finally he ended the matter by saying, "Except I shall see in his hands the print of the nails, and put my finger into the print of the nails, and put my hand into his side, I will not believe." Here the minute particularity of details shows that Thomas takes up what the disciples had said. Thomas affirms that he will not believe unless he has the same experience that the disciples claimed to have had, with the addition that he wished to test the sense of touch as well as that of sight. He wished to handle this ghost to learn if his eyes deceived him. This decision seemed a hard one to the disciples, who were full of their new faith and joy. And yet Thomas could reply that there was too much at stake to have false hopes revived. He had gone through the collapse of his hopes. He did not desire to have another downfall. Besides, optical illusions were possible. The mind might even project images before the eyes like the mirage of the desert. He wished to have a real scientific examination before he could believe.

It cannot be said that Thomas differed essentially from the position of the disciples before their experience on Sunday night. True, he had their testimony to add to that of the women. But they signally failed in the power of convincing Thomas of the reality of their experience as we to-day, alas! so often fail to convince sceptics of the power of Christ. He held out longer than the rest, and demanded the same proof that they asserted had convinced them with a certain tone of superior intelligence that often goes with a sceptical attitude toward Christ. It is the vice of the professional sceptic that he assumes an air of intellectual arrogance toward those whom he considers the dupes of their own credulity. Thomas probably prided himself on his refusal to be carried away by what looked like a case of nerves on the part of both men and women who actually believed it possible for Jesus to appear to them. And yet Thomas had seen Lazarus come out of the tomb. Perhaps he argued that it was Jesus who raised Lazarus and now Jesus was dead. Besides, Lazarus went on living his old life with his human body. He was not a mere ghost who came into a room with closed doors. Hence Thomas wished to be able to handle Jesus before he could believe in his resurrection.

Had Thomas demanded too much? Have we a

right to make a material test for spiritual phenomena and experiences? Many a man has stumbled right here and has not known how far to go and where to draw the line between material science and the things of the spirit. But Thomas was not holding himself aloof from the disciples because of his scepticism. We do not know why he failed to be present the first Sunday night, when he missed so much. If he had known that Jesus would come he surely would have been on hand. There are those to-day who miss the blessing because they are not with God's people when the Lord makes bare the arm of his power. It is easy to expect nothing from the gathering of the people of God. There was no promise that Jesus would meet with the disciples on the second Sunday night. But Thomas was present this time. It was not hard to get him to come. His own curiosity would bring him, and he was probably urged to come. If anything out of the way happened he would at least be there so as to form his own opinions concerning what took place. Thomas has the scepticism of inexperience that afflicts so many to-day. Those who have not felt the power of Christ in their own lives may find it hard to believe that Christ touches the lives of others. So Thomas comes to their second gathering in a critical mood and on the watch against any hallucinations or clap-trap. He had not long to wait before Jesus appears, the doors being closed as before, and challenges the doubt of Thomas with the words: "Reach hither thy finger, and see my hands: and reach hither thy hand, and put it into my side: and be not faithless, but believing" (John 20:27). It was all so sudden that the shock

upset Thomas's programme of examination. He knew
the voice of Jesus. He knew that familiar and dear
face. There were the outstretched hands and the side.
But Thomas did not put his hand into that wounded
side. In a crisis faith has to act and to decide. Faith
is higher than knowledge. Faith has various sources
of knowledge. It uses the intellect, the affections, and
the will. The intellect is arrogant at times and seeks
to rule out the affections and the will, but they have
to be heard. We must use our intellects, for God gave
them to us. But he also gave us our affections and our
will. Thomas really understood no more than he did
before how Christ came into that room, and how he
rose from the dead, but here Jesus was and Thomas
must decide what to do and at once. Thomas sur-
renders to the Risen Christ: "My Lord and my God"
(John 20:28).

This is no mere exclamation of amazement, as the
reply of Jesus shows. Thomas gave Jesus the worship of his heart and Jesus accepted his new faith and
loyalty at its face value. We do not have to say that
Thomas fully grasped the significance of his language
and comprehended how the Risen Christ is both God
and man. Faith has risen above mere intellect ever-
more. Faith has seized upon the heart of the situation. The man who has struggled with his honest
doubts has risen by faith of experience to the noblest
confession in the Gospels. It is Thomas the doubter,
the pessimist, the sceptic, who has become the man
of sublime faith. We may thank God that it is possible for such a thing to happen. Jesus was patient

with Thomas, for he knew that he was not posing as a sceptic for social prestige, but at heart really longed to believe. He was not occupying a false position, but was working toward the light. So Jesus met Thomas with proof that won him. But Jesus puts no crown on the doubt of Thomas. He rejoices in his new conviction and frank confession, but Thomas has missed the highest form of faith. He had refused to believe in the Risen Christ unless he conformed to his own test. He had refused to believe the witness of those who had seen the Risen Christ. So Jesus says: "Because thou hast seen me, thou hast believed: blessed are they that have not seen, and yet have believed" (John 20:29). This beatitude Thomas has missed. It belongs to those who will never see with their eyes Christ on earth, but who will be satisfied with the testimony of the eyes of the heart. They will reach up the hands of faith and will grasp the hidden hands of Christ. These are the heroes of faith who do not make unreasonable demands of Jesus in the realm of the Spirit.

Surely this rebuke to Thomas may be a rebuke to-day to those who press their scepticism too far. Criticism and science have their rights and their duties, but the intellect is not the whole of man any more than the body is the whole of life. The kingdom of God consists in love and joy and peace and righteousness, and not in meat and drink. Peter heard Jesus speak this rebuke to Thomas. And Peter will one day speak of Jesus, "whom having not seen ye love; in whom, though now ye see him not, yet believing, ye rejoice with joy unspeakable and full of glory" (1 Peter 1 :8). That blessed privilege is open to every believer to-day whatever doubts may beset him. He can find his way back to Christ—in whose face one finds the glory of God.

CHAPTER XII

PHILIP THE EVANGELIST

Luke calls him "Philip the evangelist one of the Seven" (Acts 21:8). The two epithets cover very well what we know of his career. It is here seen that the Seven had come to occupy a place to themselves after the fashion of the Twelve. They were chosen, as is shown in Acts 6:1-6, to relieve the Twelve of "serving tables" whatever that may mean. Our word "banker" means originally a "bencher" because the money-changers sat at tables. So Jesus overturned the tables of the money-changers in the temple (John 2:15). Thus to serve tables probably means to attend to financial affairs. In the present instance the business concerned the distribution of the funds for the poor widows among the saints in Jerusalem. The Hellenistic Christian Jews of the Dispersion who were in the city complained that the Aramæan (Palestinian) widows received more than their share of the money. The Twelve Apostles had supervised the equitable distribution of the funds. At once they saw that to continue this duty would jeopardise their spiritual functions and prejudice the Hellenists against them. So they wisely asked the Hellenists to choose seven of their own number for this special task. This provision would allow the Twelve freedom to devote themselves to prayer and the ministry of the Word. It is not

certain that the deacons described later in Phil. 1:1
and 1 Tim. 3 are identical in office with the Seven;
but all the indications point that way. The word
"serve" (*diakoneo*) employed in Acts 6:2 and deacon
(*diakonos*) are identical in root. One possible etymology derives the word from *dia* and *konis* (dust),
meaning to raise a dust. Certainly some deacons can
fill that requirement. The word has a wider applica-
tion in the New Testament to ministers in general, and
all service for Christ. But the office of deacon to
which Philip was appointed was designed to relieve
the Apostles (and elders a bit later) of the more secu-
lar phases of the work of the churches.

So Philip began his career as a church official as
one of the Seven, a deacon. He was a loyal sup-
porter of Stephen, the leader of the Seven, when
Stephen took the lead in the aggressive interpretation
of the spiritual nature of Christianity as designed for
men of all races. The sudden martyrdom of Stephen
for this wider vision of the mission of Christianity
did not frighten Philip. The Twelve Apostles had
aroused the bitter hostility of the Sadducees by their
bold proclamation of the fact that Jesus had risen from
the dead and the guilt of the Sanhedrin from his cruci-
fixion. Stephen stirred the Pharisees to fury by his
apparent denial of the necessity of the Jewish ceremonial law for Gentiles. Philip took the death of
Stephen as a challenge to his own faith and courage
and did not hesitate to take up the work of Stephen.
It remains one of the puzzles of the early apostolic
history why the apostles did not rally to the support
of Stephen and Philip in their vigorous campaign.

Did they feel that they were going beyond the functions of the Seven? Or did they think it unwise for them to antagonise the Pharisees too much as well as the Sadducees? Or did they feel that the Seven were going too fast toward the Gentiles? We have no means of answering these questions. We only know that Saul's persecution finally drove all the disciples out of Jerusalem except the apostles. Stephen and Philip are not the only deacons who have taken to preaching. They were set apart as members of the Seven (Acts 6:6). There is no evidence that they received any further "ordination." To the end Philip is one of the Seven. In modern ecclesiastical language they were lay preachers like D. L. Moody. But for the moment Stephen and Philip took the lead in aggressive evangelisation.

It is interesting to note that Philip went to Samaria as Luke tells us in Acts 8, the chapter devoted to the work of Philip. It may have been that he was safer from persecution in Samaria than in Judæa or Galilee as the Jews had no synagogues in Samaria and no dealings with them. The Samaritans had been finally circumcised, but the Jews refused to consider them as a part of their own people. They were half-Jews and were all the more cordially hated for that very reason as people to-day have an extra touch of spite for their own kindred in a family fuss. The striking thing is that Philip boldly applied the teaching of Stephen and followed the example of Jesus who had himself preached with marked success in Sychar (John 4). True, Jesus had once forbidden the Twelve to go into any way of the Gentiles or into a city of the

Samaritans (Matt. 10:5) while on the special tour
of Galilee. But, before he ascended on high, he expressly charged them to be his witnesses in Judæa and
Samaria and the uttermost part of the earth (Acts
1:8). It is possible, as one tradition has it, that Philip
was one of the Seventy sent forth also by Jesus (Luke
10:1-24). But Philip, like Stephen and all the Seven,
was a Hellenist while the Twelve were all Palestinians.
So he had less difficulty in overcoming race prejudice.
He is the first missionary of the Cross on record who
carried the gospel message to an alien race.

Philip had power with the people as he kept on
preaching Christ to the people of the city of Samaria.
The multitudes (note the plural, the crowds) gave heed
to (held their minds on) the things that were spoken
from time to time by Philip. He had caught their
ear and had a hearing and they hung on his words.
This they did with one accord. He carried the crowd
with him as they heard him speak and watched the
signs that he wrought. Like Stephen (Acts 6:8)
Philip wrought miracles. Unclean spirits were cast
out. Paralytics were healed. The lame walked. It
was like the days of Jesus on earth again and in
Samaria. "There was much joy in that city." Perhaps the very fact that Philip was persecuted by Jews
and was an exile from Jerusalem made the Samaritans
all the more inclined to listen to his message. And
then, too, the Samaritans in Sychar had once welcomed
Jesus while the Jews later crucified him.

The great work of Philip in Samaria is all the more
remarkable in the light of the fact that they had been
led astray by Simon Magus, one of the numerous

Jewish soothsayers and exorcists (cf. the seven sons of Sceva in Acts 19 at Ephesus). The Magi (cf. the visit of the Wise Men to Jerusalem and Bethlehem to do honour to the New-born King) were originally great and wise men of much lore and insight. But as some doctors are quacks and some preachers are hypocrites, some of the Magi became magicians or tricksters who played on the ignorance and superstition of the masses. So here this man Simon had his repertoire of stunts by which he fooled the people and convinced them of his claims to be "some great one" (*Magus* means *great one* originally). He continually astonished the people by his new "powers" and held the population in awe from the smallest to the greatest. He was almost worshipped as "the Power of God that is called Great." It is pathetic, really tragic, to see how otherwise intelligent men can become the victims of charlatans in religion and in politics. Even Sergius Paulus was under the spell of Elymas Barjesus in Cyprus and many a modern man has sought communication with spooks by the help of mediums in darkened chambers like Saul with the Witch of Endor. In our own time Mrs. Eddy has claimed to be some "great one" superior to Jesus Christ and some have followed her hallucinations as Alexander Dowie has founded a city on his own absurdities. But Philip broke the spell of the power of Simon Magus over the people. Simon saw that his "power" was gone. He was a fallen idol. At once he himself became a follower of Philip in order to get the benefit of the new "cult" which had put him out of business. Luke records that "Simon himself believed and was baptised and kept close to

Philip and beholding the signs and great powers taking place continued amazed." This language tells
the secret as the sequel makes plain enough. Simon
"believed" that he wanted what Philip had. He submitted to baptism as a magical rite akin to those in
the various cults of the times. He thought that, if
he were baptised, he himself would be able to work
the wonders that Philip continued to perform. But,
somehow the "power" did not come to Simon. So he
kept close on the heels of Philip to see if he could
catch on to the particular spell or incantation by which
he supposed the miracles to be wrought. He is the
typical case of the man who joins the church for what
he can get out of it and without any spiritual experience of grace or change of heart. Baptism to Simon
was not a symbol of the grace already received, but a
magical means of obtaining the power to work
miracles.

It is small wonder that, when the apostles in Jerusalem heard that Samaria had received the gospel, they
sent at once Peter and John to investigate the situation.
The Samaritans, as already stated, had been circumcised and so could not be treated as heathen in the
spread of the gospel. And yet race prejudice and
race hatred .made .it wise for the apostolic leaders to
look the situation over to avoid trouble in Jerusalem.
Peter is the very one who later had the vision on the
housetop at Joppa and who preached to Cornelius and
his family in Cæsarea and had these Romans baptised and who was called to account by the Pharisaic
element in the church in Jerusalem. John was one
(James the other, Luke 9:54) who wanted to call

down fire from heaven to consume a Samaritan village
that would not receive Jesus because his face was set
toward Jerusalem. And in Jerusalem one of the mean-
est things that his enemies could say of him was that
he was a Samaritan and had a demon (John 8 :48).
But here both Peter and John approve the work of
Philip, a tribute to the skill with which Philip had
carried on his work, and they prayed that the converts
might receive the Holy Spirit. Philip was not hypersensitive or jealous and was apparently glad to see
Peter and John. One recalls how later Barnabas was
sent from Jerusalem to investigate the conversion of
the Greeks in Antioch in Syria and how he remained
with joy till the work was well established.

The outpouring of the Holy Spirit in Samaria was
virtually a Samaritan Pentecost distinct from conversion and apparently accompanied by speaking with
tongues as in Jerusalem and at Cæsarea. Suddenly
Simon Magus "saw" a great light and felt that at
last he had caught on to the incantations of laying on
of hands, provided it would work for him as it did for
Peter. So he boldly offered Peter money for his gift,
treating him as a fellow conjurer who was out for
the money. It was an intolerable affront and Peter
scorned him and his money and warned him that he
was in the gall of bitterness and the bond of iniquity,
without part or lot in this thing, with a crooked heart
before God. His belief and baptism were a mere
cloak to make merchandise of the gift of God. There
is no doubt that Simon was a consummate hypocrite
and deserved the anathema of Peter. There is no
evidence of a real change of heart in him. His very

name is forever coupled with the crime of trying to purchase religious preferment and it is called simony. He was ranked as the first great heresiarch of early Christianity and legend is busy with his name in the Clementine Epistles. The germs of the later Gnosticism appear in his claims and pretensions.

Philip stands forth as a man led of God in the special mission to the eunuch of Ethiopia. He is here a prophet like Elijah or Elisha who is seized by the Spirit of God and led forth to do God's will. The Christian preacher does not claim to have the same overwhelming and clear guidance, but he is never sure and powerful when he is out of touch with God. The God-called and God-filled man is the one who has the message for men to-day. If we kept our hearts open for God's voice, we might hear the still, small voice of the Master.

The task assigned to Philip is not easy. He is to go and evangelise one man of great prominence. He is not a Jew, but probably a proselyte of the gate who has been to worship at the temple in Jerusalem. But it is always difficult to know how to handle the individual case with its own peculiar problems. Great preachers sometimes fail just here. But most men are won to Christ in precisely this way, one by one. Moody and Broadus have said that they knew of more conversions in their own experience from conversation than from preaching, great preachers as they were. Philip did not hesitate, but went on and trusted for the opening to come. He soon had it for the eunuch was reading aloud in Isaiah 53. Soon Philip was preaching Jesus from that scripture. He had no

hesitation in finding the Messiah in Isaiah as Jesus
had none. The eunuch was converted and asked for
baptism as soon as water was reached and Philip baptised him. He had evidently spoken of baptism in
his exposition of the gospel message. There was no
church at hand, but Philip did not hesitate to baptise
the new convert as Peter had the household of Cornelius baptised in Cæsarea. Ecclesiastical problems
amount to little in a time like that. Here was, besides,
a Gentile converted and baptised who went on his
way rejoicing and who probably took the message of
eternal life with him to Ethiopia as the first missionary to the heathen. No stir was raised in Jerusalem
over the case of the eunuch because Philip did not go
to Jerusalem, but went to Azotus and then to Cæsarea
where he made his home. But he preached as he went
and evangelised the cities of the plain on the way. He
deserves the title of the Evangelist.

It is over twenty years before we hear of Philip
again. Paul is on his way to Jerusalem for the last
time. Paul and Luke with the rest of the party reach
Cæsarea on their way to Jerusalem to take the money
from the Gentile churches to the poor saints in Jerusalem. They stop at Cæsarea as guests of Philip and
his four daughters who are prophetesses, a wonderful
home of Christian activity, a dynamo of spiritual
energy. It is plain that Luke made full use of his opportunity in this home at this time and later when
Paul is a prisoner in Cæsarea to obtain data for the
early part of Acts. But it was a strange meeting of
rich and varied reminiscences for Paul and Philip.
Paul was the leader in the persecution that killed Ste-

phen and that drove out Philip the successor of Stephen. And now Paul and Philip meet again after long years of service in carrying on the work of Stephen and taking the gospel to the Gentiles. Philip was the first messenger to cross the Jewish border with the story of Christ for those not Jews. Paul is the chosen vessel of Christ to the Gentile world. They have much in common and one is bound to think that these days in Cæsarea were full of fellowship and joy.

There are various legends as to what Philip and his daughters did when the war with Rome broke out in A. D. 65. It began in Cæsarea. We may be sure that they left in time and that they were useful elsewhere.

The space given Philip in Acts by Luke is not great, but it is enough to make a clear picture of one of the finest figures in Christianity. He was worthy of the friendship of Stephen and of Paul and of Luke, as well as of Peter and John. He was not responsible for the imposture of Simon Magus. Many another preacher has been taken in by designing men and women who have sought to insinuate themselves into place and power by church connection and even by the use of the pulpit. One is not omniscient and cannot always read the human heart, but time sets things straight and the hypocrite is revealed. Philip was rich in his gifted daughters who did not stand alone among women in the first century who bore noble witness to the power of Christ to save women and to enrich all that is high and holy in womanhood.

CHAPTER XIII

MATTHEW THE BUSINESS MAN IN THE MINISTRY

It is now a live question in many of the churches how to obtain suitable preachers. In some sections the supply of ministers seems to be keeping up with the increasing demand while in others there is a distressing shortage of young preachers in the schools. The reasons for the decrease on the whole are varied. The Y. M. C. A. now makes a strong pull for many of the finest young men. The foreign field has an increasing appeal for the noblest spirits in the colleges. Some young men find difficulty in reconciling the old faith with the new learning and drift into other callings. Some of the men with the new knowledge lack the conviction and the loyalty to Jesus as Lord and Saviour and so find themselves without a message and soon without an audience. There are always a certain number of failures in the ministry as in everything else. Quite a number break down under the stress and strain of the modern minister's life. Meanwhile the churches are growing and clamour for more ministers of the highest type of character and efficiency.

It is always profitable to go back to the beginning of things. In our organized Christianity we have naturally come to look to the schools for the training of the ministry. But it is actually true in some instances that the educated preacher comes out unfitted for the active ministry. At any rate it is well to understand that the churches are not wholly dependent on the schools for ministers, necessary as the schools are. God raises up men to meet special emergencies. Jesus taught the disciples to pray for more labourers to enter the harvest. Certainly there has not been enough prayer in the churches for God-sent men. God is the real source of supply for preaching of the gospel of grace. All else is secondary.

It is always possible for business men to enter the ministry. England has a large and useful number of lay-preachers who carry on their business during the week and preach on Sundays. Some of these give their whole time to preaching and at their own charges if necessary. D. L. Moody always considered himself a layman, because he was not ordained, though one of the greatest evangelists of the ages. He was a successful business man. He gave up the shoe-business to go into the soul-saving business. He carried his business attitude and habits into the service of winning souls to Christ. Successful business men need not be overlooked as a source of ministerial supply.

Jesus did not overlook them. He called a whole firm of fishermen to leave their business and follow him. James and John were partners with Simon and Andrew (Luke 5:7-10). At the call of Christ these men all left their business and devoted the rest of their lives to work for Christ (Mark 1:17-20; Luke 5:11).

But the most striking instance of the business man who entered the ministry is Matthew (Matt. 9:9), the publican who sat at the place of toll on the road that led from Damascus to Acre by the north end of the Sea of Galilee at the border between the territory of Herod Philip and of Herod Antipas. Mark (2:14) terms this man "Levi the son of Alphæus" while Luke (5:27) calls him "a publican by name Levi." Evidently the man had two Jewish names, Levi and Matthew like Simon Cephas (Peter). Probably Levi was his original name and Matthew (Aramaic "Gift of Jehovah" like the Greek "Theodore") while Matthew may have been a later name (nickname as a term of endearment or appreciation) after he entered the ministry. At any rate in the lists of the Twelve Apostles he is always called Matthew and "Matthew the publican" in Matt. 10:3. He stands seventh in Mark and Luke and eighth in Matthew and Acts.

His business was perfectly legitimate in itself, in fact necessary. Customs officers and tax collectors are proverbially unpopular and arouse a certain amount of prejudice because of the business. The Jews resented the payment of tribute to Rome and disliked any Jew who undertook to collect the duty for Rome. Matthew was technically an officer under Herod Antipas, but he incurred the dislike for his class. "Publicans and sinners" had come to be grouped together as of a piece. In many cases the publicans were guilty of graft and oppression as John the Baptist charged (Luke 3:13). Matthew was not a chief publican like Zacchæus (Luke 19:2) who farmed out a district with other publicans employed under him. Matthew simply had his customs office near Capernaum and examined the goods of those who passed along the highway and collected the dues.

To do this work he had to know both Greek and
Aramaic and he needed a certain amount of business
ability, a quick and ready turn for financial exchange
and accurate accounts. Matthew would receive the
scorn of Pharisees because of his constant associa-
tion with the Gentiles and the common run of the Jews.
Besides, he would be compelled to violate the rules of
the Pharisees concerning Sabbath observance. Jesus
himself spoke of the publicans and harlots as social
outcasts (Matt. 21:31). Matthew would not seem
to be very promising material for a preacher, least of
all for one of the Twelve Apostles. It would be like
looking for a saloon keeper to become a minister.

And yet one day in the midst of a great crowd coming and going, while Jesus was teaching them (Mark
2:13-14) and while Matthew was very busy collecting
the toll from the passing throng, the Master suddenly
said to the publican: "Follow me" (Mark 2:14).
The tense used (present imperative and so linear action) means to keep on following forever. Matthew
understood at once that it was a call to quit the customs office to go on the road with Jesus. Why did
the demand of Jesus make an appeal to Matthew? It
is quite probable that Matthew had already heard of
the fame of Jesus who now made Capernaum his head-
quarters (Mark 1:21; 2:1). The Sabbath in Capernaum when the mother-in-law of Peter was healed
closed with a great crowd. "All the city was gathered
together at the door" (Mark 1:33). It is possible that
Matthew was in that throng. The quick decision of
Matthew argues for the conclusion that he had previously faced the problem of Jesus. Now he took the

great stand in the open and made that tremendous decision. As a rule in conversion the final step is taken after a great deal of consideration in one way or another. Sermons, conversations, reading the Bible, sorrow, joy, sickness, death may all have contributed to the moment of decision. But even so the step is usually taken under the pressure of urgent invitation. When Jesus said to Philip: "Follow me" (John 1:43), Philip instantly obeyed because he "was from Bethsaida, of the city of Andrew and Peter" (1:44). We follow the example of others whom we know and love.

It was not easy for Matthew to yield to the command of Jesus in spite of the charm of the Master for men. Matthew had no other means of livelihood so far as we know. Jesus was an itinerant rabbi with no fixed income. For the moment he was the popular idol, but one could not know how long it would continue to be so. Matthew himself came from a class that was taboo with the religious leaders of the time. His coming would apparently embarrass Jesus and not help him. But he took his stand for Jesus openly and boldly. He rose up and followed Jesus then and there (aorist tense in Mark 2:14 and Matt. 9:9) and he kept on following him (imperfect tense in Luke 5:28). Matthew was not a quitter. He had counted the cost. He "left all," Luke adds. Jesus does not demand that every business man give up his business and enter the ministry. But he does ask that of some. A successful business man cannot assume that he is not to receive a call to become a preacher. His very success in business may be one of his qualifications

for the ministry. It used to be said that preachers were
not good business men, but, if the average business
man had to support his family on the income of the
average preacher, he would be slow to make that statement. And certainly modern business men feel as
never before the need of preachers to help them apply
the teaching of Jesus to the economic problems of the
world. The Wall Street Journal openly affirms that
the greatest need of the business world to-day is more
religion and righteousness. Business men in the ministry would help greatly in making a bond of contact
between Christianity and business.

Matthew not only took a public stand for Jesus
before the business men of his day. He made a strong
appeal to his business associates to become disciples of
Jesus. "And Levi made a great reception for him in
his house : and there was a great multitude of publicans
and of others who were reclining at meat with them"
(Luke 5:29). Luke makes it plain that it was the
house of Levi and not of Jesus as the language of
Mark 2:15 and Matthew 9:10 allows. But Mark and
Matthew note that the crowd of "others" were "sinners." Mark explains that many sinners "were following" Jesus. Matthew asserts that "many publicans
and sinners came and reclined with Jesus and his disciples." But Luke makes it clear that Matthew invited the crowd of "publicans and sinners," social outcasts like himself, his own friends and associates.
Some of these "sinners" may have come uninvited.
It is possible that Matthew may have accumulated a
little money. At any rate he was anxious to show
his colours. The only people who would accept an in-

vitation to a reception were his own acquaintances and associates. The courage of Matthew is beyond all praise. So often Christian business men are shy in their testimony for Christ when they make a loud noise in business circles. Matthew wanted his old friends to meet Jesus. He was sure that they also would like him. It is plain also that Jesus was already known as willing to mingle with these social outcasts for they eagerly gathered round Jesus and gladly accepted Levi's invitation.

Matthew was willing to incur ridicule for Jesus. The scribes and the Pharisees noticed the big crowd at the house of Levi the publican. They were already showing an interest in the teachings of Jesus as a rival for popular favour (Mark 1:22). They were not themselves invited by Levi and they would have spurned his invitation if it had been extended. But they had no hesitation in standing outside the house and making remarks about the conduct of Jesus in eating with publicans and sinners. "Why does your teacher eat with publicans and sinners?" (Matt. 9:11). They clearly mean to imply that their teachers would be ashamed to eat with such people. Take notice that "they were murmuring" (Luke 5:30). It was like the buzz of bees. This pointed criticism in public was embarrassing to Matthew who had given the feast. There was nothing that he could say, for the crowd of publicans and sinners were his invited guests. The disciples did not feel like speaking though the question was addressed to them. Jesus took up the criticism and made a pointed rejoinder that is given verbatim by all the Synoptic Gospels: "The well have no need of a physician, but the unwell." It is not hard to imagine the electric effect of this piercing saying of Jesus. Jesus was already the great Physician of body and soul. Surely the publicans and sinners needed the physician of souls. The Pharisees and scribes posed as physicians of souls, but they dodged the very people most in need of their services. Jesus had a further word for them: "But go and learn what *this* means: I desire mercy and not sacrifice" (Matt. 9:13). This was a thrust at the whole fabric of Pharisaism. The sarcasm of Christ appears in his closing word: "For I have not come to call righteous folks, but sinners to repentance" (Luke 5:32). He took them at their own estimate as "righteous" and brushed them aside. They were intermeddlers at Levi's reception and in the work of Christ. Certainly Matthew would appreciate the powerful word of defence from his new Friend and Lord. Matthew was getting his first experience of that public criticism that every preacher must endure who does anything worth while. The preacher has to learn how to take criticism, to profit by it, to throw off much of it, to go on with his work in spite of Madame Grundy. "They say?" "Let them say."

We have no reason to think that Matthew was a man of unusual gifts. Certainly he had not spectacular gifts that made him an outstanding figure in the new circle of Christ's disciples. He was not called on this occasion to be one of the Twelve Apostles, but to join the group of four fishermen who were already following Jesus (Andrew and Simon, James and John). Two others (Philip and Nathanael-Bartholomew) had already cast in their lot with Christ and the four. Five of these seven had been business men and that may have been true also of Philip and Nathanael. But the absence of any particular mention of Matthew apart from the rest in the later story in the Gospels indicates that he was on a level with the group as a whole and not a genius and not a distinctive leader. He was not clamorous for the first place in the Twelve as were James and John, Peter, and Judas Iscariot. But Matthew can at any rate be credited with the quality of steadiness and steadfastness. He apparently had not been a follower of the Baptist as the six first had been. He was then a newcomer in the circle and would not be likely to claim any particular honours or expect any special favours. The great feast that he gave in honour of Jesus was a hearty expression of his gratitude to the great Teacher and perhaps also in some sense a jubilation or celebration of the new departure in his own career. Matthew had certainly made a daring leap from the post of publican to that of preacher of righteousness. But Jesus knew that Matthew was a publican when he called him. He knew the cleavage between the Pharisees, the ceremonial separatists of the day, and the publicans and sinners who outraged all the social and religious conventions of the Pharisees. Jesus deliberately took his stand by the side of "sinners" who repented as against the pride of the self-righteous whose hearts were full of hate for the down-trodden among men.

It is not certain that Matthew comprehended fully the significance of the spiritual, moral, and social revolution of which he was a part. He was called upon to play a not ignoble part in the great drama of all time. For one thing he had to prove the wisdom of Christ in calling a publican instead of a Pharisee. He had to overcome by a clean and straight life in the sharpest and bluntest criticism. His own life in all probability had not been above reproach. He had most likely lived up to the reputation of his class as an oppressor of the poor and as a grafter. This he had to overcome by a clean and straight life in the open. Jesus tested Matthew by some months of constant fellowship and service with the other six. Matthew came to understand better what lay ahead of him. So it came to pass that after a night of prayer in the mountain Jesus came down to a lower plateau and chose the twelve men whom he named apostles who were to be his cabinet of co-workers for the kingdom of God. He chose "Matthew the publican" in that fateful number of men on whom so much depended. As a general rule it is wise for any man to have some testing or trial before he fully launches into the ministry of Christ. It is not always an easy thing to manage for the churches are usually shy of a novice in the ministry. A man cannot learn to preach without preaching. He must practise on somebody. In the case of young men who have to spend years of preparation for the work the decision usually has to be made on the basis of promise and faith. It is a chance in futures from the human standpoint. My own experience as a theological teacher for some thirty-five years may be worth something. Probably over five thousand young ministers have been in my various classes during these years. I am often asked what percentage of these students fail to enter the ministry. I have kept no accurate data, but my general impression is that the actual loss is less than two per cent of the whole. To be sure, those that come to the theological seminary have usually had high school and college training. Most of them have already had student pastorates or regular pastoral work. The love of preaching has already gripped them. The work in the Southern Baptist Theological Seminary has deepened their love for souls and for soul-winning. I am glad to be able to bear this witness to the loyalty of the great host of the noblest of men whom my life has touched by the grace and goodness of God. These men have become good ministers of Christ, in varying measure, to be sure, but still with honourable fidelity and with a measure of the favour of God upon their work. They have girdled the earth with lives of consecrated toil for Christ. I thank God to-day for the holy and happy memories connected with them. So Matthew, the former publican, took his place with the elect group of choice spirits chosen by Jesus for fellowship in service, his earthly bodyguard in the midst of misunderstanding and relentless and increasing hostility.

One other thing can be affirmed with confidence concerning Matthew. Papias in the well-known passage in Eusebius is quoted as saying that Matthew wrote Logia of Jesus in Hebrew (Aramaic) which each one interpreted as he was able. Tradition credits him with the authorship of our First Gospel, the canonical Gospel according to Matthew. The present Gospel according to Matthew bears little mark of being a translation from Aramaic. It seems to be a free composition in Greek, free at least in the same sense that the Gospel according to Luke is free, with the evident use of materials such as Luke mentions (Luke 1:1-4). It is not my purpose here to enter into a discussion of the Synoptic Problem, the broad outlines of which are now pretty generally accepted. My own views are fully stated in my books ("Commentary on Matthew in the Bible for Home and School," "Studies in Mark's Gospel," "Luke the Historian in the Light of Research"). Both Matthew and Luke make use of Mark's Gospel and a non-Markan source commonly called Logia or Q (German Quelle, Source). This non-Markan source may very well have been the Logia of Matthew mentioned by Papias. Since Matthew was bilingual as a publican at his post near Capernaum on the great West Road, it is quite possible that he may have written the Logia in Aramaic and the Gospel in Greek. But, leaving that point to one side, there is every reason to think of him as one of the very earliest narrators of the things of Jesus Christ. Some scholars even hold that Matthew began to take notes of the sayings of Jesus Christ during the Master's ministry. If so, the Logia of Jesus by Matthew took shape some twenty years before the Gospel of Mark which reflects so faithfully the vivid pictures seen by Peter. The point is made that Matthew's habits as a customs officer led him to jot down, perhaps at first in shorthand, notes of the wonderful words that fell from the lips of the great Teacher. If there is anything at all in this hypothesis, we find in Matthew an illustration of one's business habits bearing fruit in the ministry. The Gospel according to

Matthew has been termed the most useful book in the world, for it is the book about Jesus that has been most read. It has given most people their conception of Christ. Even if Matthew did not write the Greek Gospel bearing his name, his Aramaic Logia made a great contribution to the picture of Jesus. It is likely that the Logia was much larger in content than the non-Markan element in both Matthew and Luke as we can judge by the use made of Mark's Gospel. And in the absence of definite proof against the Matthæan authorship of the First Gospel, his connection with it must be considered possible, some would say probable, and that is my opinion.

There are many legends concerning the preaching of Matthew, some of them certainly confused with Matthias. These may all be passed by in our estimate of the work of Matthew for Christ. If he had done nothing else but write the Logia of which Papias spoke and which modern criticism finds in large measure preserved in our canonical Matthew and Luke, he would be entitled to the rank of one of the benefactors of humanity. The group of twelve men whom Jesus gathered round him challenge our interest from every standpoint. Each had his own gifts. The veil of silence rests upon the work of most of them. We are able to form a fairly clear picture of Peter, John, Judas, and Matthew, with a fainter outline of Philip, Andrew, and James. Perhaps few in the circle would have thought of the solid and more or less stolid Matthew as one who would win immortal fame. But work counts in the end of the day fully as much as genius. The greatest men have both genius and the capacity for work. In fact, genius is largely a capacity for work. But the less brilliant minister can do an honest day's work with the gifts that he has in the place where God has placed him. These are the men who must meet the demands of the new world. Every man must plough his own furrow to the end and must make it as straight as he can and make it fit in with the work of others. Christ calls upon business men to-day either to enter the ministry or to back up the ministry with personal service and with money to make Christianity effective in the life of the world.

CHAPTER XIV

JUDAS THE TRAITOR TO HIS LORD

The case of Judas is the saddest of all those who came in contact with Jesus during his earthly ministry. Others sinned grievously, but Judas sinned against more light than they all. Simon Peter denied his Lord under sudden impulse when caught in the toils of circumstance, but Judas sinned with deliberation and calculated treachery. Pilate sinned against Roman law according to his own confession, but he palliated his conscience like some other politicians by laying the blame upon the Sanhedrin. The sin of Caiaphas was greater than that of Pilate as Jesus said (John 18:11). The Sanhedrin gleefully accepted their share of the guilt for the death of Jesus (John 19:7) while the populace enthusiastically exclaimed: "His blood be on us and on our children" (Matt. 27:25). There was guilt enough for all. Sadducees, Pharisees, and Herodians buried the hatchet against each other for the moment in order to vent their spleen against Jesus, the common object of their hatred.

But Judas stands out above all the rest as the supreme example of treachery for all time. His very name, though one of the commonest and most honourable in ancient Jewish history (merely the Greek form of Judah) became the synonym for all that is base and mean. Benedict Arnold can only be called a second Judas. "The enormity of the sin of Judas consisted in its being against all bonds of discipleship and friendship; against light, against mercies, affection, trust, warning; against his own promises and preaching" (Plummer in Hastings's "D. B."). Keim argues that it is impossible to think that the treason of Judas would have been invented if he had not been guilty. With all the minute research into the details of the life of Jesus in the Gospels no serious effort has been made to show that Judas did not betray his Lord. And Judas does not stand alone in the history of Christianity though he does head the list of traitors. A few men who once preached the glory of Jesus have lived to curse his name to the end.

There have been those who sought to relieve Judas of real blame for his conduct by various specious arguments. The commonest plea is that he was the chosen vessel to betray Jesus so that he could die for sinners, that it was God's plan that Christ should die on the Cross and that this could only happen by betrayal to the Sanhedrin because of Christ's power with the people. But this explanation handles in too light and easy a manner the whole problem of the origin of evil and of human responsibility. There is no real ground for saying that Judas was put among the Twelve Apostles in order that he might betray Jesus. Certainly Jesus did not say that he selected Judas because he knew that he would betray him. It is not clear from John 6:64 that Jesus meant to say that he knew who would betray him from the beginning of his own ministry. He may mean only that in the early stages of the work of Judas he saw signs that

Judas was given over to the work of the devil and would betray him. That is clear to Jesus one year before the end (John 6:70), though the exposure seems not to have shocked the Twelve at that time. Already the heart of Judas was with those who walked no more with Jesus (John 6:66).

Some would even make Judas a sort of hero in that he tried out of excess of patriotism and loyalty to force the hand of Jesus and compel him to be king in open rebellion to Cæsar. The idea is that Judas disliked the refusal of Jesus to respond to the pupular clamour in Galilee a year before his death (John 6:15). The triumphant entry gave Jesus a great following, but even so he showed no purpose to follow it up in a political way. If Jesus were in the hands of the Sanhedrin, the people would rally to his standard and throw off the Roman yoke. So the argument runs, but it is very feeble and inconclusive and overlooks too many items that demand explanation, especially the fact that Jesus calls him a devil (John 6:70).

Others argue that Judas was wholly evil without any element of good, that he even sought out a place among the Twelve in order that he might have an opportunity to betray Jesus. Beyond doubt Judas early fell into the power of the devil. Both Luke (22:3) and John (13:27) say that Satan entered into Judas just before the betrayal and, as we have seen, Jesus called Judas a devil a year before that. Evidently, therefore, the connection of Judas with the devil was no new and sudden thing. In fact John (13:2) observes that Satan had "already" put the notion of betrayal into his heart. It is clear, therefore, that Judas had for some time brooded over his dark project in secret communing with the devil. Probably at first the suggestion was more or less unconscious, but finally he was fully aware of his own purpose and welcomed the periodic visits and impulses of Satan in his heart. Undoubtedly Judas played with temptation until finally he became the tool of the devil who wrought his own will through him. But in the last analysis that is the story of many a sordid life. The worst dope fiend became a degenerate by degrees. There was a time when resistance was possible.

Judas had elements of good in him that appealed to Jesus. "Ye did not choose me, but I chose you and appointed you that ye should go and bear fruit, and that your fruit should abide" (John 15:16). And Jesus thanked the Father for giving him these twelve men (John 17:6): "And I guarded them and not one of them perished, but the son of perdition" (John 17:12). But "the son of perdition" brought that fate upon himself, Jesus clearly means. The Master early perceived the elements of peril in Judas and began to warn him in subtle ways and then more openly. But these warnings against hypocrisy probably at first passed by undiscerned. When they became more personal, they were probably bitterly resented as "flings" and proof of Christ's dislike for Judas. It is hardly likely that Judas would take to himself the general denunciation of covetousness and hypocrisy or even the implication that the light in any of them might be darkness (Luke 11:35). When Jesus spoke of one of them being a devil (John 7:70), Judas may have passed the epithet on to others, as

people will a hit in sermons. And when at the end
the language of Jesus was unmistakable, Judas was
simply confirmed in his purpose to go on with his
hellish bargain. "Ye are clean, but not all" (John
12:10). "He that eateth my bread lifted up his heel
against me" (John 13:18). When Jesus pointedly
said at the last supper: "One of you shall betray me,
even he that eateth with me" (Mark 14:18), the other
disciples were sorrowful and amazed and looked on
one another to see if they could see signs of such
treachery in each other (John 13:22). When each
asked "Is it I," Judas did the same thing brazenly
(Matt. 26:25). He would bluff it out as long as he
could, though he now knew that Jesus understood him
thoroughly. The disciples actually questioned each
other on the subject (Luke 22:23), but failed to grasp
the significance of the sign when Jesus gave the sop
to Judas as he indicated in response to John's question to Jesus and the suggestion of Peter (John 13:23-
26). It is even possible that Judas got the post of
honour at this last feast, a circumstance that would
blacken his character still more. But Judas understood perfectly the language of Jesus: "What thou
doest, do quickly." He was now wholly in the grasp
of the devil and the warnings of Jesus apparently only
exasperated him to go on to the end.

It is not possible to explain the career of Judas by
one motive. It is not possible to explain the conduct
of any ordinary man in that way. Jesus was in complete
fellowship with the Father. He was both God and
man, but the Father's will ruled his life. Of no one
else can that be said in that sense. Mixed motives

control most men and women in what they do. That
was certainly true of Judas. We may put it down as
certain that he did not consciously set out to be a
traitor. He was undoubtedly drawn to Jesus at first
by the charm of his words and by the nobility of his
character. Like the other apostles he brought the
Pharisaic conception of a political Messiah with him
and he held on to that in spite of the teaching of Jesus
to the contrary. It was not till the great Pentecost
that the rest saw the truth about that fundamental
point. Judas was dead by that time. It is possible to
trace some of the motives that led Judas astray.

Ambition was undoubtedly one of them. It is quite
likely that he thought of himself as the leader of the
twelve. In Mark 14:10 the best manuscripts call
Judas "the one of the twelve." We know that they
had several disputes on that very point as to which was
first. Simon Peter felt himself the natural leader of
the group because of his ready speech and impulsive
character. At Pentecost after the Ascension of Jesus
he did take the lead. Jesus was the real leader while
on earth. James and John openly demanded the two
best places for themselves, a selfish request that stirred
the indignation of the rest. During the last year of
his ministry Jesus took pains to explain to the disciples
the spiritual nature of his kingdom and by degrees
the fact of his death in Jerusalem. Peter openly rebuked Jesus for speaking in such a despondent way of
his death and brought upon himself the epithet
"Satan." All this slowly sank into the heart of Judas
and disappointed ambition rankled in his breast. He
grasped firmly the conviction that he cared far more

for a certain place in a new political revolution than for shadowy hopes about a spiritual and heavenly kingdom. After the glory of the triumphal entry on Sunday morning it must not be overlooked that on Tuesday morning in the temple Jesus made open breach with the Sanhedrin and made it impossible for the religious leaders to accept him as Messiah. On the Mount of Olives Jesus had delivered an extended discourse full of woe and disaster for the city and the world. Pessimism evidently gripped Judas powerfully at the turn of events. He may have desired to save what he could out of the wreck.

Jealousy also played its part beyond a doubt. Judas was the only apostle from Judæa. The rest were from Galilee. This fact would tend to make him suspicious about little things. At the last supper there was an unseemly scramble for the place of honour next to Jesus. It is not certain who got it, whether Judas, Peter, or John. But we do know that the wrangling continued during the feast, after all had reclined, to such an extent that Jesus arose and took a basin of water and a towel and began to wash the disciples' feet to give them an object lesson in humility. Wounded pride heals slowly. Judas may have felt that Jesus suspected him and would honour the others, men of inferior powers, in preference to himself. So he would come to justify himself in his own feelings toward Jesus.

Undoubtedly Judas felt resentment at the public rebuke given him by Jesus at the feast at the house of Simon the leper. Judas made the protest against the apparent waste of money by Mary for the ointment

(John 12:5). To be sure, his mention of the poor was a flimsy protest, but all the other disciples instantly joined in and supported Judas in his criticism of Mary (Mark 14:4; Matt. 26:8). The rebuke of Jesus was direct and manifestly cut Judas to the quick. The breach between Judas and Jesus was now wide open. Jesus appreciated sentiment and love and even spoke of his death in this connection (John 12:7). Judas was practical and selfish and thought chiefly of what he could get out of his allegiance to Christ. He had followed Christ in the ups and downs of his ministry. He had seen him the hero of all Galilee and had done his share to arouse Galilee when the twelve toured the land by twos. He had preached Christ's gospel of the kingdom and had cast out demons. He had gone with Jesus when a practical refugee from Galilee and had seen the gathering storm in Jerusalem. He had done his part to turn Jesus away from the folly of a complete breach with the Jewish leaders in Jerusalem. This public rebuke before all the twelve and the other guests he considered an unforgivable insult. It was the last straw on the camel's back. He left the feast at Bethany in disgust and went straight to the Sanhedrin and offered to betray Jesus to them (Mark 14:10). He acted as if in hot resentment, but it was not a new thought. Satan entered into him afresh at this juncture (Luke 22:3), but he was now merely ripe fruit for the devil's hand.

Covetousness played its part also in the ruin of the soul of Judas. John notes that Judas was a thief and had been in the habit of pilfering from the company bag that he carried for all (John 12:6). But John's comment is made in the light of the after development. At this stage no one of them suspected him of financial crookedness. He was the treasurer of the company and had won this place of responsible leadership because of business ability and a practical turn for affairs. He no doubt felt that, as treasurer of the group, he had a right to file a protest against the reckless and foolish extravagance of Mary in the waste of so much money on mere sentiment. They had not had too much money and often were in want with nowhere to lay their heads. But for the handful of women who ministered to them of their substance (Luke 8:1-3) their condition would have been much worse. The covetousness of Judas appeared to him as economy and good business sense. Many another has excused his own stinginess by polite terms of like nature. The love of money cheapens a man's whole nature and does much to destroy the finer qualities. At any rate Judas seems blunt and brutal as a spy before the Sanhedrin: "What are ye willing to give me, and I will deliver him unto you?" (Matt. 26:15). It is hard to believe that even a miser would have come over to the enemy for so small a price as thirty pieces of silver which the chief priests weighed out unto him in advance (Matt. 26:15). It was the price of a slave (Exodus 21:32) and that fact would give added pleasure to Judas in his mood of angry resentment and disappointed ambition. He acted probably on impulse in going all of a sudden to the Sanhedrin to make the proposal to show them how to seize Jesus during the feast in spite of the multitude of adherents that he had (Luke 22:6). But he stuck to his nefarious bargain with deliberation and pertinacity. He had plenty of opportunity to change his mind and to return the money. On the other hand "he sought opportunity" to deliver Jesus to the Sanhedrin.

So the shameful compact was carried through to the letter. Judas came back and took his accustomed place with the eleven who suspected nothing to the end. They even misunderstood Christ's last word to Judas before he left on his hellish mission as a message about his duties as treasurer (John 13:29) even after Jesus had exposed the betrayer to them all. They did not have eyes to see such treachery. Judas was a coward like most criminals. He knew the real power of Jesus and came to the Garden of Gethsemane, Christ's favourite place of prayer, and took advantage of his knowledge of Christ's habits of piety (John 18:2). But even so he came with a band of soldiers and with lanterns and torches and weapons (John 18:3). Judas felt the power of Jesus in the bold challenge and the manifestation of the supernatural power (John 18:4-9). But there was no turning back now. Judas had crossed the Rubicon. There was no need for him to go on with his sign to the soldiers to identify Jesus. He was already marked out by his own conduct. But Judas kissed Jesus excessively (Mark 14:45), adding insult to injury. The last word of Jesus to Judas made it plain that he was understood (Matt. 26:50).

The remorse of Judas was in keeping with all the rest. It was not real repentance, but only sorrow at the outcome. After the actual condemnation of Jesus Judas began to see himself in his true light. The blur of anger and resentment subsided enough for him to see his own portrait. That has often happened with a murderer or a rapist after the deed is done. Gloating satisfaction gives place to a reviving conscience that whips like a scorpion sting. So in a rage he rushed to the chief priests and confessed his crime: "I have sinned in that I have betrayed innocent blood" (Matt. 27:4). But they were not interested in that phase of the subject: "What is that to us? See thou to it" (Matt. 27:5). He flung the pieces of money into the sanctuary, where he was not himself allowed to go and departed.

There are two accounts of the death of Judas, that in Matthew 27:4-10 and that in Acts 1:18-19. They differ in several details and are probably independent traditions. It is possible to harmonise them if one wishes to do so. He may have hanged himself and have fallen down, the rope breaking, and burst asunder. The field could have been called the field of blood because his own blood was shed on it and also because the Sanhedrin bought it with blood money, the price of the death of Jesus, and so have used it as a potter's field for burying strangers. At any rate the chief priests apparently took the money that they had spurned but used it for this special purpose. There are legends about his death that may be passed by.

The greatest Tragedy of the ages carried with it the treachery of Judas and the faltering of Simon Peter, two of the leading apostles. In fact, they all deserted for a time and fled like sheep without a shepherd as Jesus had said they would. But Peter sincerely repented and came back and made good. But

Judas went over the cliff. He went down with the Niagara flood. Peter says that "he went to his own place" (Acts 1:25). He went to his doom that he had earned for himself. We are all caught in the womb of circumstance and at times we seem the victims of destiny that we cannot control. But our spiritual destiny we make for ourselves. Terrible as was the fate of Judas, one must conclude that he had in him the making of a great preacher of Christ's gospel. Jesus saw the good that was possible in Judas as he did in Simon. But Simon, in spite of his ups and downs, became at last a rock, while Judas became a devil. Both were under the tutelage of Jesus. Both had the same privileges. Both were men of weakness and frailty. One fought the devil after momentary defeat. The other courted the devil and listened to his blandishments.

Judas carries a perpetual warning to every preacher of Christ. Paul saw the peril clearly: "I therefore so run as not uncertainly, I so fight as not beating the air, but I beat my body and keep it in subjection, lest, after having preached to others, I myself should become rejected" (1 Cor. 9:26-7). Paul warned us not to give place to the devil (Eph. 4:27). Others can tread under foot the Son of God (Heb. 10:29) and crucify him afresh and put him to an open shame (Heb. 6:6). It is a high and holy privilege to be allowed to come into the inner circle of Christ's followers. It is a dread catastrophe to see such a one sink back into the pit from which he was digged. It were indeed good for that man if he had not been born (Matt. 26:24).

CHAPTER XV

DIOTREPHES THE CHURCH REGULATOR

The Elder who writes the Third Epistle of John was probably the Apostle John, the Beloved Disciple of the Fourth Gospel, and the author of First and Second John. He does not call himself John or an apostle, but that proves nothing. Peter terms himself "a fellow-elder" in writing to "the elders" (1 Peter 5:1). The style of the three Johannine Epistles is the same as that of the Fourth Gospel. Not all scholars agree, to be sure, but we may think of the aged Apostle John writing these letters in his zeal to help on the mission work in Asia Minor. In the later years of the first century the story is that John lived at Ephesus where Paul had laboured for three years and where later Timothy was Paul's loyal disciple in charge of the evangelistic work. Already Gnosticism had come into this region to play havoc with the churches as we see in Colossians and in the Pastoral Epistles. This subtle heresy concerned itself primarily with a philosophical theory that all matter is essentially evil. This theory, like that of Mrs. Eddy that matter is non-existent, involves serious consequences in morale and in doctrines. In particular, it involved a degrading view of the person of Christ, like "Christian Science" again. Two forms of Gnosticism appeared. One, the Docetic, denied that Jesus had a

real human body at all. "For many deceivers are come
forth into the world, they that confess not that Jesus
Christ cometh in the flesh" (2 John 7). These here-
tics held that Jesus was an *æon* or intermediate being
between God and man and only seemed to have a human
body. The other view, that of Cerinthus, was that
Jesus the man and Christ the *æon* that came on Jesus
at his baptism were different, curiously like the "Jesus
or Christ" controversy in the *Hibbert Journal Sup-
plement* (1909). "Who is the liar but he that denieth
that Jesus is the Christ?" (1 John 2:22). The churches
were rent by this heresy. Some went out (1 John
2:19), while others remained in the membership.

There were loyal missionaries going among the
churches. These had to be entertained and supported.
John urges Gaius to "set forward on this journey
worthily of God" (3 John 6) these brethren and
strangers withal, "because for that for the sake of the
Name they went forth, taking nothing of the Gentiles" (verse 7). One is reminded of the directions
of Jesus to the Twelve Apostles when they were sent
over Galilee by twos. So Paul and his co-labourers
journeyed over much of the Roman Empire. So missionaries to-day go through Central China. The treatment of these heralds of the Cross became a test of
one's loyalty to Jesus as missions is to-day a touch-
stone of vital Christianity. "We therefore ought to
welcome such, that we may be fellow-workers for the
truth" (verse 8). The least that a true Christian could
do was to give hospitality for these pioneer preachers
who pushed on to the harder fields. There were few
hotels in our modern sense of comfort and the public

inns were usually impossible places because of vermin (human and non-human). So hospitality was a Christian virtue of the first quality as it still adorns many a home to-day.

It is not certain whether Diotrephes was a Gnostic or not. It seems pretty clear that he sympathised with that doctrine. Some of the Gnostic propagandists were fierce in their denunciations of Christ and of Christianity. Cerinthus and John were held to be strongly antagonistic. It would come to pass that one could not show hospitality to a Gnostic without being suspected of sympathy with that heresy. "If any one cometh unto you, and bringeth not this teaching (the teaching of Christ), receive him not into your house and give him no greeting" (2 John 10). Such an extreme course could only be justified where the heresy was very radical. To-day one might hesitate to give hospitality to a Mormon missionary or to a professional or blatant infidel.

John says: "I wrote somewhat unto the church" (3 John 9). Both Gaius and Diotrephes were apparently members of the same church, though what church we do not know. That letter to the church is apparently lost, though some scholars see it in 2 John (the elect lady), an unlikely supposition. This lost letter dealt with the proper reception of the missionaries as they went from church to church. This letter probably covered much of the same ground as the Third Epistle to Gaius, urging the right reception of Demetrius and of the other brethren who were doing good for God. It may be questioned whether this letter to the church contained formal denunciation of Diotrephes, though that is possible. Certainly John was not afraid of Diotrephes, for he was not afraid of Cerinthus.

But our Third John is a private letter to Gaius sent at the same time as the public epistle to the church. Probably the main point in this letter is to warn Gaius about Diotrephes. In this private letter probably John employs language a bit sharper than in the other. John is evidently anxious that Diotrephes shall not be allowed to prejudice the church further against him and the missionary brethren. He wishes Gaius to forestall such action on the part of Diotrephes. But the letter is a frank testimonial to the power of Diotrephes in the church of which Gaius is a member. It is to be a struggle between Gaius and Diotrephes for mastery in the church, between the evil and the good. "Beloved, imitate not that which is evil, but that which is good. He that doeth good is of God: he that doeth evil hath not seen God" (3 John 11). We need not draw the conclusion that Diotrephes is wholly evil, but certainly his influence is dangerous for the cause of Christianity. He is still a member of the church and exerts great power over the church as will be seen.

The precise ecclesiastical position of Diotrephes is not clear. Some have seen in his exercise of power the monarchical bishop of later times. That is an unnecessary hypothesis in the absence of any evidence of bishop as distinct from elder (presbyter) in the New Testament as Lightfoot has shown. It is not absolutely certain that Diotrephes was an elder or bishop at all, though that is likely. Probably both Gaius and Diotrephes were elders in the same church as we see several elders at Ephesus and Philippi. It is possible that Diotrephes was a deacon. Many years ago I wrote an article for a denominational paper concerning Diotrephes. The editor told me afterwards that twenty-five deacons had ordered the paper stopped as a protest against the personal attack in the paper. What I did in the article was to show that Diotrephes was a typical church "boss" who ruled the church to suit his own whims. In Kentucky we have a phrase termed "the short-horn deacon" for this type of church regulator. I once heard of such a deacon who boasted that he had made every pastor leave that he had ever had. To be sure, a preacher can be a church "boss" as well as the deacon. But it is easier to drive the pastor away than the deacon. I know of one case where the pastor quietly informed such a deacon that he (the deacon) would have to go if anyone left. The deacon left and joined another church.

The sin that John charges against Diotrephes is that he "loves to have the pre-eminence." The word here employed by John is a very rare one and means "fond of being first." A late *scholion* explains it as "seizing the first things in an underhand way." The word occurs among the ecclesiastical writers to picture the rivalries among the bishops of the time. It is a sad commentary on human nature that even preachers of humility often practise the pushing of self to the front in an unbecoming spirit and manner. One recalls that once Jesus found the disciples disputing among themselves who was the greatest among them, a spirit that Jesus sternly rebuked by placing a little child, possibly Peter's own child, in the midst of them, and by saying that the greatest was the one who served the most. And once James and John with their mother actually came to Jesus with the formal request that they be given the two chief places in the kingdom of Christ (the political Messianic kingdom of their expectation). And at the last passover meal Jesus had to rebuke the apostles for their unseemly conduct in scrambling for the post of honour at the meal. It was with this peril in mind that Jesus urged the apostles to love one another and prayed for unity among them and among all his future followers. Ambition is not sinful in itself though our very word (of Latin origin) had a bad history, for it suggests politicians who would take both sides of an issue in order to get votes. This double-dealing is due to the desire for place and power. Jesus noted that the Pharisees loved the chief seats in the synagogue in order to be seen of men. Their piety was particularly punctilious if enough prominence could be obtained to justify the display and outlay of energy. A certain amount of ambition to excel is good for one. Ambition is a good servant, but a bad master. It is dangerous for ambition to have the whip handle in one's life. Diotrephes loved the first place among the brethren. He was determined to be first at any cost. If any honours were to be bestowed, he assumed that they belonged to him as a matter of course. He must be consulted on a matter of church policy else he was against it. The least detail of church life must receive his sanction else he would condemn it. If he was not chairman of all the committees, he must be regarded as an *ex officio* member. If Diotrephes had been the sole pastor of the church, something could be said for such pre-eminence. But evidently Gaius was also one of the elders. And Diotrephes may have been only a deacon. But the spirit of a man like Diotrephes does not depend on office. Such a man rates himself as the natural leader of the church by reason of his native gifts, family, money, reputation. The only way for the church to have peace is for all freely to acknowledge this brother's primacy. Plutarch notes that Alcibiades wanted the first place. He got it and he ruined Athens by the expedition to Syracuse. It is impossible to calculate the harm that has been wrought in the churches by church dictators like Diotrephes.

Diotrephes drew the line on John. He "receiveth me not." He refused to recognise the standing and authority of John the Elder and Apostle. The word here rendered "receive" occurs in the papyri in the sense of "accepting" a lease and in Maccabees 10:1 for "accepting" a king. Evidently Diotrephes treated John as a heretic or as John is said to have treated Cerinthus when he rushed out of the bath when Cerinthus came in lest the house fall in because of God's wrath. One recalls the temperament of this "son of thunder" who came to be known as "the apostle of love." It was John who in great zeal reported to Jesus one day: "Master, we saw one casting out demons in thy name; and we forbade him, because he followed not with us" (Luke 9:49). But Jesus rebuked John's narrowness of spirit about method of work. "Forbid him not: for he that is not against you is for you" (Luke 9:50). John and James were those who asked Jesus to call down fire from heaven to consume the Samaritans who "did not receive"

Jesus (Luke 9:52-55). But Jesus "turned and rebuked them." John was now the aged apostle who
went from church to church with the message: "Little
children, love one another." But he still had the old
fire and vigour with more justification against Diotrephes than against the examples in the Gospel of
Luke. Diotrephes was turning the tables on John
(cf. 3 John 10) and was refusing to recognise or to
entertain John as a genuine minister of Christ. Besides, he said slighting things about John, "prating
against us with wicked words." The word translated
"prating" occurs as an adjective in 1 Timothy 5:13
"tattlers" (*verbosæ, Vulgate*). These idle, tattling
busy-bodies excited Paul's disgust. That is John's
word for Diotrephes. He seemed to have John on the
brain and gadded around with idle tales and "wicked
words" derogatory to John's character and work,
seeking to undermine his influence for good. This
sort of propaganda against preachers is only too common. It degenerates into idle gossip. One of the
saddest spectacles in modern Christianity is to see
the very forces that are designed to co-operate with the
pastor in pushing on the work of the kingdom of God,
engaged in pulling down all that the pastor and other
church members try to do. The result is the paralysis
of the work and the mockery of the outsiders who sneer
at Christian love and unity. As a rule the pastor
can only suffer in silence and go on with those who
have a mind to work in spite of the slackers and the
hinderers. Silence is the best answer to idle slander.
But sometimes the man of God has to speak. And then
it should be to the point and very brief and in a way

to help the cause of Christ, not to do harm. As a rule, well-doing is the best way to put to silence the ignorance of foolish men (1 Peter 2:15). John does not mind ostracism by Diotrephes save as that leads others astray.

But Diotrephes draws the line on all of John's followers. Diotrephes was "not content therewith." He was not satisfied with his vindictive opposition to John the Elder. "Neither doth he himself receive the brethren." Probably these missionary brethren had letters of commendation from John. That item would only anger Diotrephes all the more. It was now his habit to close his door against anybody aligned with the Apostle John. He will not recognise the Elder. He will not recognise the followers or co-labourers of the Elder. Hence John pleads with Gaius to take special interest in those who "for the sake of the Name went forth" (3 John 7). One recalls the language of Luke in Acts 5:41, "Rejoicing that they were counted worthy to suffer dishonour for the Name." This way of referring to Jesus became common, it is clear. The problem of welcoming those who travelled from place to place and who claimed to be at work in the name of the Lord was a vital one for a long time as is seen in "The Teaching of the Twelve Apostles," XII, 1: "And let everyone that comes in the name of the Lord be received and then after testing him ye will know." The brother who claimed to be for the Lord had the presumption in his favour, but some wolves travelled in sheep's clothing and a certain amount of discretion was called for then and now. Even to-day, with all our publicity and modern facilities for information, people are only too often taken in by slick-tongued adventurers who make money out of gullible brethren and sisters and then move on to fresh pastures. There is some advantage in having some sort of a line drawn. John is not here demanding that Diotrephes reform, but that Gaius see to it that John's missionaries are taken care of when they come. One of my clearest childhood memories is that of Elias Dodson, a quaint and godly missionary of the old Home Mission Board of Southern Baptists. This gifted and consecrated man went from house to house on his mule and usually had only one suit of clothes. He used to ask for a dollar for the Indians and he generally got it. He would write postcards ahead about his entertainment or send little notes to the denominational paper concerning his appointments and entertainment. He was a modern example of John's travelling missionaries from church to church. Elias Dodson did much to create a real missionary spirit in Virginia and North Carolina. Even those who were opposed to missions found it hard to put a ban on Elias Dodson and his mule.

But Diotrephes sought to dictate to the whole church a line of conduct toward John and his missionaries. "And them that would (receive the brethren) he forbiddeth and casteth them out of the church." Here we see the rule or ruin policy of the church "boss." This self-willed leader is not content that he shall be allowed to treat John and his missionaries as outsiders. He demands that everyone in the church do the same thing. He had the whip handle in the church and was determined to force his will upon the entire membership. It is not clear whether he actually succeeded or not. The tense in the Greek allows merely the threat and the attempt for "casts out." In John 9:34 the Pharisees actually "cast out" (aorist tense) the blind man who stood out against them that Jesus was not a sinner, but a prophet of God. They turned him out of the synagogue and then Jesus met him and saved him, a grotesque picture of a synagogue that fought against God in Christ. If Diotrephes actually compelled this church to expel those who dared to welcome the missionaries of John, it was an honour to be outside of that church. But the fact that Gaius was still a member of the church, an elder apparently, argues for the conclusion that Diotrephes was simply terrorising the brotherhood by his threats. But it was bad enough for a church to have a "bulldozer" like Diotrephes who blocked the path of progress for the church. He had become the chief liability to the church instead of its chief asset.

So John exposes Diotrephes plainly to Gaius. John is not afraid to face Diotrephes. He is anxious to do so, but he cannot come yet. Meanwhile, he puts Gaius on his guard and urges him to break the power of Diotrephes over the church by daring to show him up as he really is. Gaius owes this duty to the church. But John hopes to come some day. "Therefore, if I come, I will bring to remembrance his deeds which he does." One needs only to read 1 John 2 to see how plainly John can speak when the occasion calls for it. It becomes a sad duty sometimes to expose the wicked ambition of a man with the rule or ruin policy. It is better that such a man drop out of the church than that the church wither and die. Our churches need leadership, but not domination. The difference is vital. Leaders lead, bosses drive their slaves under orders.

CHAPTER XVI

EPAPHRODITUS THE MINISTER WHO RISKED
ALL FOR CHRIST

All that we really know about Epaphroditus we learn from Paul's Epistle to the Philippians, but that little is exceedingly suggestive and helpful. The name is the same as the shortened form Epaphras that appears in Colossians 1:7; 4:12; Philemon 23. But there is no likelihood that it is the same person, for Philippi and Colossæ are quite too far apart for the same man to be a messenger from both cities to Paul in Rome at about the same time. Besides the name is a· not uncommon one on the inscriptions. So we must rely on Philippians 2:25-30 and 4:10-18 for all our knowledge of his life and work. But these passages furnish us a reasonably clear picture of a bold and courageous personality who hesitated not to do his simple duty in the face of great difficulty and even of peril. In this respect he is a fine example of thousands of loyal ministers of Christ who have done the work of the hero with none of the halo that comes to many men in other callings of life. The call for the heroic still appeals to the best type of young men who enter the ministry of Jesus Christ. Many of these suffer in silence and in poverty at home and die like martyrs on the foreign field. It is all in the day's work with these men, true soldiers of Christ.

Epaphroditus was the messenger of the church in Philippi to bear the gifts of this noble church to Paul while in Rome. This church was the very first that gave Paul actual financial help in his missionary propaganda as Paul expressly states (Phil. 4:15-16). At first Philippi stood alone among the early churches in this "fellowship" or "partnership" (*koinonia*) with Paul. Paul greatly appreciated this active participation with him in his campaign to win the Gentiles to Christ and he mentions it a number of times (Phil. 1:5, 7; 2:30, 4:15). They had come to Paul's help several times before while in Thessalonica (Phil. 4:16) and in Corinth also at a time when Paul was in actual want (2 Cor. 11:7-10) because the church at Corinth was critical and suspicious and not generous. So once again after some years the church at Philippi has blossomed out ("sprouted up," Phil. 4:10) again with a rich reminder of their love for Paul, a sweet aroma that was pleasing to God as well as to Paul (4:18) and that God alone could reward with His riches in grace. Paul terms Epaphroditus, the bearer of this gracious bounty, the church's "apostle" (*apostolos*), or missionary. It is the same word that he applies to the "apostles of the churches" (2 Cor. 8:23) who were associated with Paul in the gathering of the great collection for the poor saints in Jerusalem. It is the original and general meaning of the word that appears in a technical sense when applied to Paul the Apostle and to the Twelve Apostles. But Paul does not hesitate to call Epaphroditus "your apostle." He is also "your minister." Here the word (*leitourgos*) is the same as our "liturgy." It means one who does work for the people and had more than the modern ceremonial sense, though it recalls the service of the priests in the temple service and ritual.

In fulfilling this special mission to Paul Epaphroditus was filling up what had been lacking in the ministry of the Philippian church for some years (Phil. 4:30). They had loved Paul all the while. He knew that. But they had lacked opportunity to show their unchanging love for Paul the founder of their church. But now that long imprisonment has befallen Paul they manage to have some share in the alleviation of Paul's tribulation (Phil. 4:14). So Paul puts it down in his column of credits to this church (4:15), once the only church with such a column. Epaphroditus did his part in the transaction nobly and Paul received the gifts.

But Epaphroditus fell sick on his arrival in Rome. The voyage was a long one for those days, unless he came partly by land to Brundisium and on to Rome. But travel had its risks on land even with the fine Roman roads. The inns were poor and robbers were numerous. But the enemy that attacked Epaphroditus was apparently the terrible Roman fever (violent malaria) that is still a peril to strangers when they come. The attack was apparently sudden. "For indeed he fell sick nigh unto death" (Phil. 2:27). It is one of the speculations of the moderns about Greece and Rome that the mosquito did as much as the barbarian to bring down these great peoples of the past. Only the hardiest could survive malignant malaria. The illness of Epaphroditus was evidently prolonged for the report of it reached Philippi and the news came back to Epaphroditus that his friends in Philippi had heard that he had fallen sick (Phil. 4:26).

The effect of this information upon Epaphroditus, who was now a convalescent, was very depressing. He was like a college boy who is ill and who hears how distressed his mother is because of his illness. Epaphroditus was now longing to go back as soon as his strength permitted. Paul implies that he was homesick by his weakness and absence from home. Paul had come to be very fond of Epaphroditus. He probably had him in his own hired house as much as he could. He certainly visited him often. He calls him "my brother and co-worker and fellow-soldier." Paul does not use the term "fellow-prisoner" so that Epaphroditus suffered no hardship of that nature because of his service to Paul who was allowed to receive his friends freely (Acts 28:30-31). But Paul had come to love this "fellow-soldier" who had incurred such peril "for the work of Christ" (Phil. 4:30). He feared that he would have "sorrow upon sorrow" like the waves that pile up on one another when the billows roll over us. That fate seemed to be Paul's, but God had mercy upon Epaphroditus and upon Paul and spared this brave soldier of Christ. So Paul is grateful and glad.

But the close call, as we say, of Epaphroditus raises the question of how much risk a preacher should take in doing his work for Christ. Certainly no minister is justified in neglecting the ordinary precautions of health. He has no right to assume that God will make him immune against disease because he is a preacher of the gospel if he violates the customary

rules of hygiene. Some ministers eat too much and
exercise too little. They have nervous headaches as
a result and lose sleep and keep irregular hours. They
expose themselves unduly and unwisely when overheated after preaching. They rush out into the cold
air with heated respiratory organs. On the other
hand some preachers are overcautious and "molly-
coddle" themselves and become hypersensitive by
wearing too heavy clothing and living in overheated
rooms. Some preachers are the victims of quacks and
patent medicines, not to say dope, and are the dupes
of scheming adventurers. But, when all is said, it is
the duty of the preacher, to have a healthy body to do
the Lord's work, if he can have it. But many a delicate man has wrought a long and laborious work for
Christ by taking proper care of himself. John A.
Broadus was such a man. But the problem raised by
the case of Epaphroditus is whether the preacher
should take known and foreseen risks to do the work
of Christ. Paul says that Epaphroditus literally
"gambled with his life" (Phil. 4:30). The word used
is our *parabola* which was employed of the gambler's
dice. Certainly Epaphroditus knew of the peril of
the Roman fever. But then other men went to Rome
on business and on pleasure. So to-day drummers
for American tobacco companies go to China and for
gain go to Africa. Physicians risk their lives every
day to save human life. Should not preachers risk
theirs to save human souls? When the yellow
fever epidemic was last in New Orleans, Dr. D. I.
Purser, one of the Baptist pastors, was away on his
vacation. He boldly came back to minister to the

sick and to bury the dead.   He stood at his post and,
before the scourge was over, fell a victim to the plague
and died.   He lost his life and saved it.   To-day no
name is more honoured in New Orleans than that of
David Ingram Purser, Sr.   It is the spirit of the true
soldier and Epaphroditus was Paul's "fellow-soldier."
The soldier cannot falter where the path of duty lies.
Once that is plain, there is no alternative.   Each man
must bear his own cross whether it be a personal afflic-
tion or a call to go into the valley of death.   It is good
to think that the ministry to-day is not without men
of the heroic spirit who quietly and simply meet the
hard demands of their calling.   There are some quit-
ters, some slackers, some deserters, some few traitors,
alas.   But the great body of modern ministers measure
up to the high standard of Epaphroditus as men who
are willing to risk all for the work of Christ.   They
do not do it for the sake of notoriety, but for the love
of Christ.   In the early centuries these "riskers" were
called *parabolani,* men who missed the martyr's death,
but who deserved the martyr's crown, for they stood
in their places and did a full man's duty in the hour of
peril.   It was this spirit in the pioneer preachers of the
United States that laid broad the foundations of
American liberty and life.   The missionaries to-day
exhibit it in numerous instances.   It is seen in some
of the "sky pilots" at home who do hard work with
little recognition among men.   Many a country
preacher has measured up to the ideal of Epaphroditus.
He has done a great work in a small place and that
is better than a little work in a big place.

Paul is now sending Epaphroditus back to Philippi.

He had hoped to come himself ere long and still cherishes that purpose when once he is free again. He cannot spare Timothy just yet. So Epaphroditus is going back and that gives Paul the occasion to write this most beautiful of all his wonderful Epistles, a letter of the utmost delicacy and insight, sympathy and elevation of sentiment. There will be triple joy in his going. Epaphroditus will be happy, the Philippians will rejoice to see him again, and Paul will be less sorrowful by reason of their joy. The keynote of the letter is joy in Christ and Paul is exuberant in spite of many untoward circumstances. The secret of happiness Paul has learned by now and he finds it in the constant fellowship with Christ, not in the changing outward conditions of his environment.

Paul makes a plea that the Philippians receive Epaphroditus with all joy. It would seem to be hardly necessary to make that request, but Paul leaves nothing undone that will add to the happiness of Epaphroditus who had done so much to fulfil the wishes of the Philippians and to add to Paul's comfort. His daring and his sufferings had endeared him all the more to both Paul and the Philippians. He deserves special honour for his work's sake. He had been a hero of the Cross as truly as Alvin York and Sergeant Woodfill deserve recognition for their prowess in France. "Hold such in honour," Paul urges, "because for the work of the Lord he came nigh unto death, risking his life that he might fill up what was lacking in your service to me." We can easily conjecture the joy of the greeting given Epaphroditus when he arrived and delivered Paul's gracious letter of gratitude which was read to the whole church. They would recognise the same dauntless spirit that sang praises at midnight in the Philippian jail.

It is fitting that a plea be made that due honour be given by the churches to their ministers who live and labour for the work of the Lord. In most instances the plea is not needed for these pastors receive the full love and loyalty of an appreciative and a devoted people. In a few cases the minister is not worthy of special honour because he has not given himself wholly and heartily to the work of the Lord. People are keenly sensitive to slackers in the ministry. As a rule, these men sooner or later drop out. But sometimes zealous and consecrated ministers do not receive proper appreciation of their work while they are living. Their memory will be revered when they are dead, but so many people are careless and indifferent and just take for granted what needs to be expressed by word and deed. Love grows by expression. So cheer up the heart of your pastor by kind words of genuine love and by filling his larder a little fuller. Add something to his salary and so lighten the burden of family cares and set his mind and heart free to do the work of the Lord that he loves and that is so much needed.

A special word should be uttered for the old preacher who has toiled long and faithfully on a pitifully small salary. He has been able to lay by little or nothing and people no longer care for his preaching. Perhaps he is also feeble and in any case few avenues are open to him by which he can earn his living. Most denominations are now pensioning these soldiers of the Cross as a matter of simple justice. It is done by the government and by the railroads and all decent concerns for their employees. These men should not be regarded as paupers or treated as dependents. They deserve more than they will ever receive. The least that we can do for them is to give them some of the comforts of life for their old age and to give them the respect and honour that is their due. "Hold such men in honour."

There was never a time when the work of Christ made a stronger appeal to the heroic element in men than now. The tempting attractions of other callings draw away the lighthearted and the unstable. But the men who can read the signs of the times can hear the cry of China's millions for light and leading out of the grasping selfishness of the nations that are exploiting her. The old gods of China are dead. They can no longer beat tom-toms to drive away the demons of greed that grind the nation's life beneath the modern juggernauts. The students of China feel the throb of the freedom that is in Christ. They are blindly striking out for help. The men of to-day who hear the call of Russia take their lives in their hands. And yet somebody must heed the despairing cry of a dying world. Thank God for men like Epaphroditus who have the courage to go at any cost. Plague and flood and famine only serve to challenge such men to high endeavour for the sake of Christ who gave his life that we might live and have more abundant life for others.

THE END